13th International Conference on Computational Semantics (IWCS 2019)

Short Papers

Gothenburg, Sweden
23-27 May 2019

ISBN: 978-1-5108-8761-9

13th International Conference on Computational Semantics (IWCS 2019)

Short Papers

Gothenburg, Sweden
23-27 May 2019

IWCS 2019

**Proceedings of the 13th International Conference on
Computational Semantics - Short Papers**

23–27 May, 2019
University of Gothenburg
Gothenburg, Sweden

Introduction

Welcome to the 13th edition of the International Conference on Computational Semantics (IWCS 2019) in Gothenburg. The aim of IWCS is to bring together researchers interested in any aspects of the annotation, representation and computation of meaning in natural language, whether this is from a lexical or structural semantic perspective. It embraces both symbolic and machine learning approaches to computational semantics, and everything in between. This is reflected in the themes of the sessions which take place over full 3 days. The programme starts with formal and grammatical approaches to the representation and computation of meaning, interaction of these approaches with distributional approaches, explore the issues related to entailment, semantic relations and frames, and unsupervised learning of word embeddings and semantic representations, including those that involve information from other modalities such as images. Overall, the papers capture a good overview of different angles from which the computational approach to natural language semantics can be studied.

The talks of our three keynote speakers also reflect these themes. The work of Mehrnoosh Sadrzadeh focuses on combination categorial grammars with word- and sentence embeddings for disambiguation of sentences with VP ellipsis. The work of Ellie Pavlick focuses on the evaluation of the state-of-the art data-driven models of language for what they "understand" in terms of inference and what is their internal structure. Finally, the work of Raffaella Bernardi focuses on conversational agents that learn grounded language in visual information through interactions with other agents. We are delighted they have accepted our invitation and we are looking forward to their talks.

In total, we accepted 25 long papers (51% of submissions), 10 short papers (44% of submissions) and 7 student papers (54% of submissions) following the recommendations of our peer reviewers. Each paper was reviewed by three experts. We are extremely grateful to the Programme Committee members for their detailed and helpful reviews. The long and student papers will be presented either as talks or posters, while short papers will be presented as posters. Overall, there are 7 sessions of talks and 2 poster sessions (introduced by short lighting talks) which we organised according to the progression of the themes over 3 days, starting each day with a keynote talk. The sessions are organised in a way to allow plenty of time in between to allow participants to initiate discussions over a Swedish *fika*.

To encourage a broader participation of students we organised a student track where the papers have undergone the same quality review as long papers but at the same time the reviewers were instructed to provide comments that are beneficial to their authors to develop their work. To this end we also awarded a Best Student Paper Award.

The conference is preceded by 5 workshops on semantic annotation, meaning relations, types and frames, vector semantics and dialogue, and on interactions between natural language processing and theoretical computer science. In addition to the workshops, this year there is also a shared task on semantic parsing. The workshops and the shared task will take place over the two days preceding the conference.

There will be two social events. A reception which is sponsored by the City of Gothenburg will be opened by the Lord Mayor of Gothenburg and will take place on the evening of the second day of the workshops and before the main conference. A conference dinner will take place in Liseberg Amusement Park where participants will also get a chance to try some of their attractions.

IWCS 2019 has received general financial support (covering over a half of the costs) from the Centre for Linguistics Theory and Studies in Probability (CLASP) which in turn is financed by a grant from the Swedish Research Council (VR project 2014-39) and University of Gothenburg. CLASP also hosts the event. We are also grateful to the Masters Programme in Language Technology (MLT) at the University of Gothenburg, Talkamatic AB and the City of Gothenburg for their financial support.

We very much hope that you will have an enjoyable and inspiring time!

Simon Dobnik, Stergios Chatzikyriakidis, and Vera Demberg

Gothenburg & Saarbrücken

May 2019

Organisers:

Local Chairs: Stergios Chatzikyriakidis and Simon Dobnik
Program Chairs: Stergios Chatzikyriakidis, Vera Demberg, and Simon Dobnik
Workshops Chair: Asad Sayeed
Student Track Chairs: Vlad Maraev and Chatrine Qwaider
Sponsorships Chair: Staffan Larsson

Program Committee:

Lasha Abzianidze, Laura Aina, Maxime Amblard, Krasimir Angelov, Emily M. Bender, Raffaella Bernardi, Jean-Philippe Bernardy , Rasmus Blanck, Gemma Boleda, Alessandro Bondielli, Lars Borin, Johan Bos, Ellen Breitholtz, Harry Bunt, Aljoscha Burchardt, Nicoletta Calzolari, Emmanuele Chersoni, Philipp Cimiano, Stephen Clark, Robin Cooper, Philippe de Groote, Vera Demberg, Simon Dobnik, Devdatt Dubhashi, Katrin Erk, Arash Eshghi, Raquel Fernández, Jonathan Ginzburg, Matthew Gotham, Eleni Gregoromichelaki, Justyna Grudzinska, Gözde Gül Şahin, Iryna Gurevych , Dag Haug, Aurelie Herbelot, Julian Hough, Christine Howes, Elisabetta Jezek, Richard Johansson, Alexandre Kabbach, Lauri Karttunen, Ruth Kempson, Mathieu Lafourcade, Gabriella Lapesa, Shalom Lappin, Staffan Larsson, Gianluca Lebani, Kiyong Lee, Alessandro Lenci, Martha Lewis, Maria Liakata, Sharid Loáiciga, Zhaohui Luo, Moritz Maria, Aleksandre Maskharashvili, Stephen Mcgregor, Louise McNally, Bruno Mery, Mehdi Mirzapour, Richard Moot, Alessandro Moschitti, Larry Moss, Diarmuid O Seaghdha, Sebastian Pado, Ludovica Pannitto, Ivandre Paraboni, Lucia C. Passaro, Sandro Pezzelle, Manfred Pinkal, Paul Piwek, Massimo Poesio, Sylvain Pogodalla, Christopher Potts, Stephen Pulman, Matthew Purver, James Pustejovsky, Alessandro Raganato, Giulia Rambelli, Allan Ramsay, Aarne Ranta, Christian Retoré, Martin Riedl, Roland Roller, Mehrnoosh Sadrzadeh, Asad Sayeed, Tatjana Scheffler, Sabine Schulte Im Walde, Marco S. G. Senaldi, Manfred Stede, Matthew Stone, Allan Third, Kees Van Deemter, Eva Maria Vecchi, Carl Vogel, Ivan Vulić, Bonnie Webber, Roberto Zamparelli

Invited Speakers:

Mehrnoosh Sadrzadeh, Queen Mary, University of London
Ellie Pavlick, Brown University
Raffaella Bernardi, University of Trento

Table of Contents

A Distributional Model of Affordances in Semantic Type Coercion 1
Stephen McGregor and Elisabetta Jezek

Natural Language Inference with Monotonicity 8
Hai Hu, Qi Chen and Larry Moss

Distributional Semantics in the Real World: Building Word Vector Representations from a Truth-
       Theoretic Model 16
Elizaveta Kuzmenko and Aurelie Herbelot

Linguistic Information in Neural Semantic Parsing with Multiple Encoders 24
Rik van Noord, Antonio Toral and Johan Bos

Making Sense of Conflicting (Defeasible) Rules in the Controlled Natural Language ACE: Design
       of a System with Support for Existential Quantification Using Skolemization 32
Martin Diller, Adam Wyner and Hannes Strass

Distributional Interaction of Concreteness and Abstractness in Verb-Noun Subcategorisation . . . 38
Diego Frassinelli and Sabine Schulte Im Walde

Generating a Novel Dataset of Multimodal Referring Expressions 44
Nikhil Krishnaswamy and James Pustejovsky

On Learning Word Embeddings From Linguistically Augmented Text Corpora 52
Amila Silva and Chathurika Amarathunga

Sentiment Independent Topic Detection in Rated Hospital Reviews 59
Christian Wartena, Uwe Sander and Christiane Patzelt

Investigating the Stability of Concrete Nouns in Word Embeddings 65
Bénédicte Pierrejean and Ludovic Tanguy

A Distributional Model of Affordances in Semantic Type Coercion

Stephen McGregor
Laboratoire Lattice
CNRS & École normale supérieure / PSL
Université Sorbonne nouvelle Paris 3 / USPC
semcgregor@hotmail.com

Elisabetta Jezek
Theoretical and Applied Linguistics
Department of Humanities
University of Pavia
jezek@unipv.it

Abstract

We explore a novel application for interpreting semantic type coercions, motivated by insight into the role that perceptual affordances play in the selection of artefactual nouns that are observed as arguments for verbs that would stereotypically select for objects of a different type. In order to simulate affordances, which we take to be direct perceptions of context-specific opportunities for action, we perform a distributional analysis of dependency relationships between target words and their modifiers and adjuncts. We propose a novel methodology that uses these relationships as the basis for generating on-line transformations projecting semantic subspaces in which the interpretations of coercive compositions are expected to emerge as salient word-vectors. We offer some preliminary examples of how this model operates on phrases involving coercive verb-object interactions.

1 Introduction

As a linguistic phenomenon that is both elusive and pervasive, semantic type coercion presents computational models with a particular challenge. The problem is to find literal interpretations of coerced phrases which tend to seem quite natural to humans, and which are correspondingly observed at a high frequency in distributional analyses of large-scale corpora.

In what follows we present an overview of the phenomenon followed by a preliminary proposal for a context-sensitive framework for interpreting predicate-object coercions. Our methodology is inspired by theoretical insight into environmental afforandances, and in this regard is in line with technical applications described in the area of image labelling by McGregor and Lim (2018). Motivated by an analysis of some of the shortcomings of a more general probabilistic approach, and also by a number of previous approaches to interpreting semantic coercion, we outline a model grounded in the distributional semantic modelling paradigm (Clark, 2015). In particular we propose a technique for constructing tensors based on an analysis of dependency relationships: this approach facilitates coercion interpretations (and conversely perhaps constructions) as geometric transformations, a move that might offer a plausible platform for capturing the direct perceptibility of environmental affordances (Raczaszek-Leonardi et al., 2018) using computational models. We present this work as an introductory overview, accompanied by a handful of examples, of a theoretically motivated methodology.

2 Background: Coercion, Affordances, and Distributional Semantics

Coercion is a theoretical tool that has been used in linguistic studies since Moens and Steedman (1988) to account for the fact that certain word combinations generate interpretations that are enriched or different from the strictly compositional ones. In the Generative Lexicon framework, predicate-argument coercion has been defined as the compositional mechanisms that resolves mismatches between the semantic type expected by a predicate for a specific argument position and the semantic type of the argument filler, by adjusting the type of the argument to satisfy the type requirement of the verb (*argument type coercion*; Pustejovsky, 1991). A classic example is (1), where *wine* is said to be coerced to an activity as a result of the semantic requirements the predicate imposes on its object, i.e. *finish* applies to an activity.[1] The implicit activity is claimed to be "drinking", and it is assumed to be stored in the lexical entry as a value of its telic *quale*.[2]

1 "When they finished the wine, he stood up".

Another line of research in cognitive and distributional semantics proposes to frame coercion in terms of thematic role fit, defined as the semantic plausibility of an argument filler to fulfil the expectation of a verb in a given role, expressed in terms of score. Thematic fit scores range from 0 to 1, and correspond to the cosine similarity to the centroid, or vector average, computed over the most typical role fillers for that verb (Zarcone et al. (2013), Greenberg et al. (2015)). Under this view, coercion is interpreted as the result of low thematic fit scores of the fillers of the argument positions of a verb rather than the response to a type clash. For example, entity-denoting objects like *wine* have a low thematic fit as objects of event-selecting verbs like *finish*, and the recovery of the implicit event is seen as a consequence of the dispreference of the verb for the entity-denoting argument. In the thematic fit approach, the retrieval of the covert event relies on general event knowledge (GEK) activation (Chersoni et al., 2017).

In our proposal, we examine the phenomenon of coercion in relation to the concept of affordance. The concept of perceptual affordances can be traced to the psychological research of Gibson (1979), who proposed that a fundamental characteristic of cognition is an agent's direct perception of opportunities for action in a particular environmental situation. By relying on the notion of affordance, we support a notion of language that, unlike the traditional symbolic view, is grounded in people's experience in their physical environment, particularly in opportunities for taking actions on objects. This approach creates a framework for interpreting the resolution of coercion as a phenomenon of semantic adjustment that relies on available affordances of objects. In fact, under this view, the possibility itself of implying a covert event in language use is understood as triggered by available affordances of objects, and the task of retrieving this implicit piece of information resides in identifying the specific affordance at play in the surrounding context.

Note that this proposal does not depart from the view that there is stereotypical information associated with lexical entries in terms of *qualia* or other means. Rather, starting with the idea that the default information encoded in words is grounded in the most relevant affordances associated with the word denotation, it examines the interaction between lexically specified information and contextually presented affordance induced by a linguistic discourse. In this paper, we focus on coercion involving artefactual objects, as we are primarily interested in modelling goal-oriented behaviour, and report the results of our first experiments towards the goal of developing a distributional model of coercion interpretation using dependency relationships between target words and their modifiers and adjuncts as the basis for generating on-line transformations that project semantic subspaces in which the interpretations of coercive compositions are expected to emerge as salient word-vectors.

3 Base Methodology: Joint Probabilities of Interpretations

Our objective is to develop a model for predicting interpretations of type coercions inherent in compositions consisting of a transitive verbs that expects an object of a certain type coupled with nouns of a different type in the object position. For the purposes of the present research, we consider an *interpretation* to be a verb that can be inserted into a coercive composition in order to resolve the mismatch between the argument type expected by the coercive verb and the type associated with the object:

2 finish the milk $\rightarrow$ finish *drinking* the milk
3 cancel the train $\rightarrow$ cancel *running* the train

As a baseline, we consider a methodology involving a probabilistic analysis of the way that both target verbs and nouns co-occur in dependency relationships with other verbs and verbals. Specifically, given

---

[1]Such cases of coercion to events are also referred to as *logical metonymies* (see Lapata and Lascarides, 2003).

[2]Recent work in Generative Lexicon claims that the *qualia* value may be updated in context and that the reconstructed event may be assigned contextually (Pustejovsky and Jezek, 2012). For example in the corpus fragment, "So unless the winemakers add tannin by finishing the wine in oak ...", the context words *winemaker*, *tannin* and *oak* trigger a different interpretation for *wine* (preparing, making) as the object of *finish*.

a target verb v that takes a target noun n as an object, we consider as candidate interpretations of the composition $v(n)$ the intersection of the set of verbs that are observed to take n as an objective argument and the set of verbals (verbs that act as nouns) that are at the head of verbal noun phrases that are objects of v. So for instance, if both the phrases *the boy drinks milk* and *the girl finished drinking* are observed, *drink* is considered a candidate interpretation for *finished the milk*.

Defining this set of k viable interpretations as R, we propose a straightforward probabilistic mechanism for assigning a score to the general appropriateness of a particular candidate interpretation $r_i \in R$:

$$s(r_i) = \frac{f(n(r_i))}{\sum_{j=1}^{k} f(n(r_j))} \times \frac{f(v(r_i))}{\sum_{j=1}^{k} f(v(r_j))} \tag{1}$$

Here $f(n(r_i))$ indicates the frequency at which the verb r_i is observerd to take the noun n as an objective argument in a corpus, and $f(v(r_i))$ correspondingly indicates the frequency at which r_i is observed at the head of noun phrases that are objects of v. Thus $s(r_i)$ can be interpreted simply as the joint probability of r_i playing the specified compositional roles with the target noun and verb.

To explore the efficacy of this scoring mechanism, we consider a list of candidate verbs and nouns:

VERBS: *finish, begin, enjoy, hear, prefer, cancel*

NOUNS: *coffee, wine, beer, milk, drink, sandwich, cake, dessert, glass, bottle, car, table, door, ambulance, train, book, newspaper, bell, radio, television*

These verbs have been selected for their tendency to coerce objects, and the nouns denote artefactual objects, which is to say, objects that have been made by humans for a reason and should presumably present a range of affordances. In order to assess the proposed metric, we extract relevant dependency relationships from the March 20, 2018 dump of English language Wikipedia.[3] A matrix composing every noun with every verb and then listing the top three interpretations in terms of the metric in Equation 1 is reported in Appendix 1.

Here we find a number of outputs that qualitatively appear to be stereotypical of the expectations for some of the more interpretable coercions. Examples include *begin [drinking] coffee, enjoy [driving] car, cancel [ordering] sandwich,* and so forth. Other cases, such as *finish [starting] newspaper,* do not seem as natural. The verb *hear* in particular appears to pose a challenge for this methodology, and it is worth noting that this verb is in a sense an outlier in that the interpretation would typically involve the action of the coerced object rather than the act of the subject upon that object: *hear* is a perception verb, and so takes an experiencer rather than an agent as a subject. So, for instance, in the phrase *hear the bell [ringing],* it is what the bell is doing, rather than what the hearer is doing, that is coerced by *hear*. There is also evidence of sense ambiguity, for instance in the case of *table,* which is across the board interpreted as something that a subject would *see*: this is presumably an artefact of a high number of mentions of tables in the sense encountered ("seen") in a document in our corpus.[4]

4   Extended Methodology: Projections Based on Syntactic Co-Occurrence

The methodology described in the previous section is largely in line with the probabilistic approach proposed by Lapata and Lascarides (2003). As those authors note, this technique does not have a facility for incorporating context into its interpretations: the sentences *the reviewer finished the book* and *the author finished the book* would be interpreted with no consideration of the different actions the respective subjects might take on a book. In the context of affordances, we can say that a book affords different sets of actions to reviewers versus authors.

A straightforward solution to this problem of contextualisation is to introduce a term involving probabilities of observing subjective arguments for candidate verbs. Compounding the score described in Equation 1 with a term for computing the probability of observing a subjective argument for the interpretive verb r_i serves both to lend context to the metric and to limit the set of candidate interpretations R. Here are three toy examples of the effect this step has on output:

---

[3] Parsing is performed using the Spacy module for Python.

[4] Word sense ambiguity in semantic type coercion is addressed in depth by Shutova et al. (2013).

4a *(brewer, enjoy, beer)*	$\rightarrow$	*produce*	4b *(patron, enjoy, beer)*	$\rightarrow$	*drink*
5a *(author, begin, book)*	$\rightarrow$	*write*	5b *(reviewer, begin, book)*	$\rightarrow$	*write*
6a *(baker, finish, cake)*	$\rightarrow$	*take*	6b *(guest, finish, cake)*	$\rightarrow$	*take*

The first pair of interpretations is qualitatively satisfying, but the second pair reveals a shortcoming in the methodology: while we may reasonably expect a book to afford reading rather than writing to a reviewer, writing is nonetheless an activity in which reviewers are categorically involved, so the high probability of observing *write(reviewer)* as a subject-predicate composition is imposed on the interpretation. The third pair illustrates the same contextual failure compounded by a tendency to offer overly general interpretations. Furthermore, instances of sentences where the subject offers such straightforward contextualisation are the exception; far more common are, for instance, pronominal subjects with removed antecedents. Straightforward syntactic heuristics are unlikely to offer a consistent way of extrapolating contexts such as subjects from sentences, to the degree that context is available at all.

To address these problems, we propose a methodology that provides a more general framework for using distributional information to generate transformations that can be performed upon a base set of representations for candidate interpretations. We begin by noting that certain grammatical classes such as adjectives and prepositions are suited to convey the affordances associated with particular objects: that a *book* might be *long* or *short*, for instance, or that something might happen *before* or *after* a *beer* suggests an aspectual quality to the actions afforded by these objects.

Following on this observation, we propose a general methodology that involves the construction of tensors based on the probability distributions associated with the co-occurrences of words in certain dependency relationships with input words.[5] These context-specific tensors can then be used to project a base set of distributional semantic representations into a subspace that captures the salient properties of a particular coercion. This idea is motivated by insight from compositional distributional semantics, where for instance parts of speech such as adjectives can be represented as matrices that transform noun-vectors to a modified representation (Baroni and Zamparelli, 2010), or where sequences of linear algebraic operations over the elements of a sentence map from word-level representations to sentence-level representations (Coecke et al., 2011).

Our conjecture is that these transformations will offer a mechanism for quantitatively encoding the affordances activated by coercions. Given a set of candidate interpretations, we can represent them in terms of their general distributional profile across a corpus (so, for instance, as a set of *base word-vectors* as described by McGregor et al. (2015)). Our objective is to transform these representations of candidate interpretations using the tensor generated by an analysis of dependency relationships, sifting the base space into a contextualised subspace. We hypothesise that geometric characteristics of the context specific subspaces will indicate apt interpretations. The norm of a projected vector, for instance, would be enhanced by the high element-wise overlap with the salient features used to define the transformation tensor, so we would expect good interpretations to drift to the outer fringe of a subspace. In order to illustrate this proposal, we offer a proof-of-concept of how our methodology can work.

A Proof of Concept For an input subject-verb-object tuple *(s,v,n)*, we consider the intersection A of all adjectives that are observed to co-occur as either a modifier of n or as a modifier of a direct object taken as an argument of the head of s. We construct two probability distributions s_A and n_A based on the L1 normalisations of the frequencies with which the words in A are observed in these relationships with s and n. We compose a vector of joint probabilities $j = \{s_{Ai} \times n_{Ai}\}$ for all $A_i \in A$ and choose the top k adjectives from A based on this metric (for the purposes of the examples here, k is set to 80). If we consider the example of *(brewer, enjoy, beer)*, then the six top scoring components that become part of A are *own*, *first*, *strong*, *new*, *local*, and *bottled*, while adjectives such as *traditional*, *seasonal*, *dry*, and *fermented* also appear in the 80 most probable co-occurrences. We extrapolate two new k-dimensional L1 normalised vectors for this set of salient adjectives, s_A^k and n_A^k, and then use the outer product of these vectors to construct a $k \times k$ tensor $T = s_A^k \otimes n_A^k$.

---

[5]Here *input words* might include a coercive dyad (such as *finish beer*), other words from a phrase or sentence, or indeed topical interpretations of a sentence, in line with the model described by Chersoni et al. (2017).

We consider the vocabulary of target interpretations I to be the intersection of all verbs that are observed to occur as both heads of n and heads of verbal noun phrases that are arguments of v, as in the methodology and examples provided in Section 3, with all verbs observed to take s as a subject. We extrapolate a set of word-vectors W_I corresponding to this vocabulary based on simple co-occurrences statistics for this vocabulary, following the skewed pointwise mutual information weighting scheme described by McGregor et al. (2015), which has been designed for the purpose of projecting conceptually contextualised subspaces of semantic representations. So, for instance, for *(brewer, enjoy, beer)*, the verb *brew* is specified as an argument observed both for *brewer* and at the head of phrases that are arguments of *enjoy*: we therefore include in W_I a vector consisting of features representing the weighting between *brew* and *own, first, new, strong*, and so on. Each vector $w_i \in W_I$ is defined in terms of the same top k elements of A that delineate T. We use T to project each word-vector in W_I into a contextualised subspace $Z = \{Tw_i : w_i \in W_I\}$.

Because the elements of T and W_I are aligned, we expect vectors with co-occurrence features that strongly correlate with the adjectives most salient to the affordances offered by n to s and activated by the coercion of n by v to emerge in Z. We measure this emergence by computing the norm for each transformed vector $z_i \in Z$ and return the vector with the highest norm as our interpretations of (s, v, n). Results for this methodology applied to the same sentences analysed above play out as follows:

7a *(brewer, enjoy, beer)* $\rightarrow$ *brew*	7b *(patron, enjoy, beer)* $\rightarrow$ *drink*
8a *(author, begin, book)* $\rightarrow$ *republish*	8b *(reviewer, begin, book)* $\rightarrow$ *bemoan*
9a *(baker, finish, cake)* $\rightarrow$ *bake*	9b *(guest, finish, cake)* $\rightarrow$ *eat*

Here we see how this methodology can inject a greater deal of contextuality into its interpretations than the purely probabilistic technique outlined at the beginning of the section. The first and third pairs are categorically plausible interpretations. The second pair is perhaps a bit stranger, with *the reviewer begins [bemoaning] the book* arguably an instance of interpreting one coercion with another, but they are illustrative of the way that a projection of candidate interpretations can expose and exploit the semantic nuance that arises in a communicative context.

5 Conclusion and Continuation

The work presented in this paper is a first attempt at developing a distributional model of coercion interpretation grounded in the theory of perceptual affordances. The idea proposed and provisionally illustrated here is that affordances can be, in a sense, simulated through an analysis of dependency relationships as observed over a large-scale corpus. This analysis has served as the basis for exploring a few examples in which interpretations are conceived of as context-specific projections from a base space of candidate word-vectors. As a first approximation, we have taken adjectives as representative of the properties afforded by particular objects in certain situations, but there is clearly scope for significant expansion of this basic assumption: we might consider other relationships observed with the coerced noun as well as head nouns in subjective roles, words observed in relationships with the coercive predicate (prepositions and intentional adverbs seem intuitively like they might be of interest here), and also words extracted using heuristics outside of dependency parsing.

It is also worth noting that an objective of our modelling approach is to provide a mechanism for representing the overall conceptual context of a sentence. Topic modelling techniques might offer a more holistic framework for the extraction of semantic cues from linguistic data, and there are various options available in this respect. A next step in this project will be the development of a dataset of sentences designed to exhibit various aspects of type coercion, and there is existing work to be considered here, for instance the dataset described by Pustejovsky et al. (2010). The development of a dataset will provide impetus for further refinement of the model itself, as there are clearly a number of directions in which this research can progress.

Acknowledgements

This work has been supported by the CHIST-ERA project ATLANTIS.

References

Baroni, M. and R. Zamparelli (2010). Nouns are vectors, adjectives are matrices: Representing adjective-noun constructions in semantic space. In *Proceedings of the 2010 Conference on Empirical Methods in Natural Language Processing*, pp. 1183–1193.

Chersoni, E., A. Lenci, and P. Blache (2017). Logical metonymy in a distributional model of sentence comprehension. In *Sixth Joint Conference on Lexical and Computational Semantics (* SEM 2017)*, pp. 168–177.

Clark, S. (2015). Vector space models of lexical meaning. In S. Lappin and C. Fox (Eds.), *The Handbook of Contemporary Semantic Theory*, pp. 493–522. Wiley-Blackwell.

Coecke, B., M. Sadrzadeh, and S. Clark (2011). Mathematical foundations for a compositional distributed model of meaning. *Linguistic Analysis 36*(1-4), 345–384.

Gibson, J. J. (1979). *The Ecological Approach to Visual Perception*. Boston: Houghton Miffline.

Greenberg, C., A. Sayeed, and V. Demberg (2015). Improving unsupervised vector-space thematic fit evaluation via role-filler prototype clustering. In *Proceedings of the 2015 Conference of the North American Chapter of the Association for Computational Linguistics: Human Language Technologies*, pp. 21–31.

Lapata, M. and A. Lascarides (2003). A probabilistic account of logical metonymy. *Computational Linguistics 29*(2), 261–315.

McGregor, S., K. Agres, M. Purver, and G. Wiggins (2015). From distributional semantics to conceptual spaces: A novel computational method for concept creation. *Journal of Artificial General Intelligence 6*(1), 55–89.

McGregor, S. and K. Lim (2018). Affordances in grounded language learning. In *Proceedings of the Eight Workshop on Cognitive Aspects of Computational Language Learning and Processing*.

Moens, M. and M. Steedman (1988). Temporal ontology and temporal reference. *Computational linguistics 14*(2), 15–28.

Pustejovsky, J. (1991). The generative lexicon. *Computational Linguistics 17*(4), 409–441.

Pustejovsky, J. and E. Jezek (2012). *Introducing Qualia Structure*. Manuscript, Brandeis University and University of Pavia, pp. 1–45. Available at https://http://gl-tutorials.org/wp-content/uploads/2015/12/GL-QualiaStructure.pdf.

Pustejovsky, J., A. Rumshisky, A. Plotnick, E. Jezek, O. Batiukova, and V. Quochi (2010). SemEval-2010 Task 7: Argument Selection and Coercion. In *Proceedings of the 5th International Workshop on Semantic Evaluation*, pp. 27–32.

Raczaszek-Leonardi, J., I. Nomikou, K. J. Rohlfing, and T. W. Deacon (2018). Language development from an ecological perspective: Ecologically valid ways to abstract symbols. *Ecological Psychology 30*(1), 39–73.

Shutova, E., J. Kaplan, S. Teufel, and A. Korhonen (2013). A computational model of logical metonymy. *ACM Transactions on Speech and Language Processing 10*(3), 11:1–11:28.

Zarcone, A., A. Lenci, S. Padó, and J. Utt (2013). Fitting, not clashing! a distributional semantic model of logical metonymy. In *Proceedings of the 10th International Conference on Computational Semantics (IWCS 2013)*, pp. 404–410.

Appendix 1

	finish	begin	enjoy	hear	prefer	cancel
coffee	serve	drink	drink	get	grow	produce
	take	grow	get	include	serve	include
	produce	serve	serve	give	drink	order
wine	produce	produce	produce	produce	produce	produce
	take	drink	drink	give	drink	give
	drink	sell	create	include	give	create
beer	produce	produce	drink	produce	produce	produce
	serve	drink	produce	give	drink	give
	drink	sell	create	sell	sell	order
milk	take	take	drink	take	take	produce
	produce	produce	take	give	give	take
	give	drink	produce	include	produce	give
drink	take	take	take	give	take	take
	serve	get	give	take	give	give
	finish	serve	get	get	buy	order
sandwich	eat	eat	eat	include	eat	order
	serve	sell	create	get	sell	include
	take	offer	get	give	serve	offer
cake	take	take	eat	give	eat	give
	eat	eat	create	take	take	take
	win	produce	take	include	give	produce
dessert	win	create	create	include	create	create
	serve	produce	eat	call	eat	produce
	eat	prepare	play	play	call	include
glass	take	wear	wear	include	wear	produce
	produce	take	read	give	take	take
	read	produce	drink	take	give	give
bottle	take	take	drink	give	take	produce
	finish	produce	take	take	give	give
	produce	drink	give	find	keep	take
car	build	take	drive	take	take	build
	take	build	take	drive	build	produce
	drive	produce	see	include	drive	take
table	see	see	see	see	see	see
	finish	turn	play	include	leave	turn
	lead	take	create	turn	keep	leave
door	open	open	open	open	open	open
	go	close	go	go	keep	close
	close	break	work	close	leave	leave
ambulance	call	call	call	call	call	call
	drive	operate	drive	include	drive	meet
	take	drive	see	drive	see	drive
train	take	take	work	take	take	meet
	run	run	take	run	work	take
	work	operate	run	see	run	run
book	write	write	write	write	write	publish
	read	publish	read	read	call	release
	publish	read	publish	call	publish	produce
newspaper	start	publish	read	tell	publish	publish
	read	tell	tell	read	read	leave
	write	sell	write	start	leave	start
bell	play	play	play	ring	play	cast
	take	take	hear	play	take	hear
	tie	ring	give	say	call	hold
radio	build	take	play	talk	leave	leave
	play	turn	do	play	play	include
	take	play	work	include	take	build
television	record	watch	watch	watch	watch	leave
	watch	broadcast	do	do	leave	watch
	write	take	play	record	do	produce

Table 1: The top three interpretations for all compositions of 6 coercive verbs with 19 artefactual objects, based on the joint probability of the interpretation occurring with each input word. The outputs *have*, *make*, and *use* are almost ubiquitously returned, and have been suppressed here.

Natural Language Inference with Monotonicity

Hai Hu
Indiana University
huhai@indiana.edu

Qi Chen
Indiana University
qc5@indiana.edu

Lawrence S. Moss
Indiana University
lsm@cs.indiana.edu

Abstract

This paper describes a working system which performs natural language inference using polarity-marked parse trees. The system handles all of the instances of monotonicity inference in the FraCaS data set, and can be easily extended to compute inferences in other sections of FraCaS. We achieve perfect precision and an accuracy comparable to previous systems on the first section of FraCaS. Except for the initial parse, it is entirely deterministic. It handles multi-premise arguments. The kind of inference performed is essentially "logical", but it goes beyond what is representable in first-order logic. In any case, the system works on surface forms and CCG parse trees rather than on logical representations of any kind.

1 Introduction

Computational systems which attempt to automate natural language inference (NLI) generally fall into one of the three categories: 1) systems which translate input into first-order logic (FOL) or higher-order logic; 2) systems based on distributional semantics, using word embeddings and then neural networks for learning inference (e.g. Bowman et al., 2015; Cases and Karttunen, 2017); and 3) systems using natural logic.

This paper is a contribution to the third category, as are Abzianidze (2015, 2017); MacCartney and Manning (2009); Angeli and Manning (2014); Angeli et al. (2016); Hu et al. (2018); Mineshima et al. (2015). Specifically, we continue work on order-based approaches to natural language inference going back to Fyodorov et al. (2003) and Zamansky et al. (2006). We make use of the polarity-marking tool due to Hu and Moss (2018). When given as input a derivation tree in CCG, this tool outputs the polarized yield of the tree. For example, when one inputs *Most Europeans live outside of Asia*, the output will be *Most$^\uparrow$ Europeans$^=$ live$^\uparrow$ outside$^=$ of$^=$ Asia$^\downarrow$*. Indeed, the tool polarizes every constituent. These arrows indicate whether inferences can be made by replacement "upward", replacement "downward", or in neither direction $=$. Iterating this idea of replacement does give a "fair amount" of inference, but to cope with NLI datasets we augment replacement with rules of natural logic (van Benthem, 1986), and with a mechanism for handling contradictions.

Our system is aimed at inference problems such as those in the FraCaS data set (Cooper et al., 1996), and we compare our efforts with the results in other papers. In addition, the ideas in our system can be adapted by others as part of their NLI toolkits.

2 Inference Algorithm

Input   A set $\mathcal{P}$ of *premises*, another set $\mathcal{K}$ called the *knowledge base* and a sentence H, the *hypothesis*.

Output   whether the relation between $\mathcal{P} \cup \mathcal{K}$ and H is *entailment*, *contradiction*, or *unknown*. The *unknown* relation means that in general, $\mathcal{P} \cup \mathcal{K}$ neither entails nor contradicts H.

Two auxilliary sets $\mathcal{K}$ and $\mathcal{S}$: a knowledge base $\mathcal{K}$ and a set $\mathcal{S}$ of entailed sentences. $\mathcal{K}$ consists of a relation $\leq$ on constituents (that is, a set of ordered pairs of words or multi-word constituents):

$$cat \leq animal \qquad kiss \leq touch$$
$$kissed\ some\ cat \leq touched\ some\ animal$$

These come from the premise set $\mathcal{P}$, or from a fixed background knowledge base $\mathcal{K}$, or from a lexical source such as WordNet (Miller, 1995). $\mathcal{K}$ also keeps track of all the nouns, verbs, adjectives, adverbs, relative clauses that appear in either $\mathcal{P}$ or H. The second auxilliary set is a *sentence base*, $\mathcal{S}$. This set stores all the inferences and contradictions our system derives, starting from $\mathcal{P}$. Inferences are stored in $\mathcal{S}.inferences$ whereas contradictions are stored in $\mathcal{S}.contradictions$. (Optionally, it might include a subset of $\mathcal{K}$ which is relevant to $\mathcal{P} \cup \{H\}$).

Algorithm The key intuition of our algorithm is that once we have a correctly polarized CCG tree, e.g., $all^{\uparrow}\ animal^{\downarrow}\ sleep^{\uparrow}$, we can replace a constituent with some word or phrase from $\mathcal{K}$ and get an inference: $all^{\uparrow}\ cat^{\downarrow}\ sleep^{\uparrow}$. This replacement is extremely simple and effective. Along the same lines, we can replace *all* with *no* to obtain a contradiction: $no^{\uparrow}\ animal^{\downarrow}\ sleep^{\downarrow}$. (This is not strictly a contradiction: in a logically-possible model, there might not be any animals. In that model, both *all animals sleep* and *no animals sleep*. However, the spirit of work in the RTE area is that we should use the more natural semantics of *all*, the semantics that carries an existential presupposition. And from this in the premise, we indeed have a contradiction.) Since we ignore most of the morphology, the words are all represented by their lemmas. We also manipulate the sentence structures so that there isn't too much variation. For example, there-be structures such as "there are NP who VP" are changed to "some NP VP". Major steps of our algorithm are listed below. (A more complete pseudocode is presented in the Appendix.)

1. Get the polarities of all sentences in $\mathcal{P}$, using the system in Hu and Moss (2018).

2. For each $P \in \mathcal{P}$: (1) Add P to $\mathcal{S}.inferences$; (2) If P is of the form "every X is a N", then add $X \leq N$ to $\mathcal{K}$; (3) If P is of the form "every X VP", then add $be\ X \leq VP$ to $\mathcal{K}$; (4) If P is of the form "N_{pr} is a N", then add $every\ N \leq N_{pr}$ and $N_{pr} \leq some\ N$ to $\mathcal{K}$.

3. Next, make the following additions to $\mathcal{K}$:

   - For each noun n and each subsective adjective a, each prepositional phrase p, and each relative clause r in $\mathcal{P} \cup \{H\}$: add to $\mathcal{K}$ the following inequalities: $a\ n \leq n$, $n\ p \leq n$, and $n\ r \leq n$. For instance, *small dog* $\leq$ *dog*, *dog from France* $\leq$ *dog*, *dog that barks* $\leq$ *dog*.

   - For each verb v, and each adverb a to $\mathcal{K}$ the inequality $v\ a \leq v$.

4. Loop over each premise P and do two types of `replacement`; one derives inferences while the other produces contradictions. See Figure 1 for a concrete example.

   - `replacement_infer`: 1) if a constituent is $^{\downarrow}$, then replace it with something "smaller" in $\mathcal{K}$; 2) if a constituent is $^{\uparrow}$, then replace it with something "bigger" in $\mathcal{K}$. Finally, store the new sentences in $\mathcal{S}.inferences$.

   - `replacement_contra`: 1) replace "no" with "some" and vice versa if the quantifier is not embedded in a relative clause[1]. 2) negate the sentence by e.g., adding "do not" before the main verb. Finally, store the new sentences in $\mathcal{S}.contradictions$.

Now the inference problem becomes a typical AI search problem. That is, we are searching for an inference that matches H string for string. If such an inference can be found before reaching a stopping criterion, then we return `entail`. If not, we turn to the generated contradictions to see if any of them matches H; if so, we return `contradict`, otherwise return `unknown`.

---

[1] "Books that *no* one reads are on the shelf" does *not* contradict "Books that *some* one reads are on the shelf".

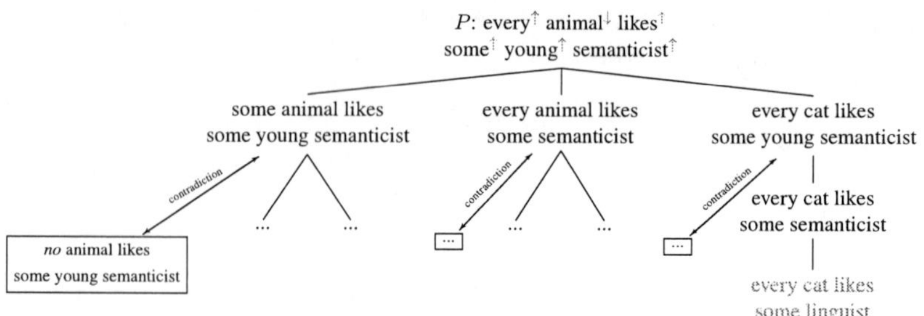

Figure 1: Example search tree where *P* is *every animal likes some young semanticist*, with the *H*: *every cat likes some linguist*. Only one `replacement` is allowed at each step. Sentences in rectangular are the generated contradictions. In this case our system will return `entail`.

Note that theoretically we can perform `replacement_infer` indefinitely, on the inferences generated in the last step. On the contrary, `replacement_contra` can only be applied once on each inference, since the contradiction of a contradiction brings us back to the premise again.[2]

This search problem is implemented using depth-first search, w/ default depth $= 2$.

Inferences not handled by `replacement`   As discussed in Hu et al. (2018), `replacement` can handle/derive many rules of natural logic, but not all of them. To name just a few the rules below are not covered by `replacement`:

$$\frac{\textit{Some y are x}}{\textit{Some x are y}} \text{SOME}_2 \qquad \frac{\textit{All (r all x) (r all y)}}{\textit{All y are x}} \text{ANTI} \qquad \frac{\textit{Det x y} \quad \textit{All x z}}{\textit{Det x (y} \wedge \textit{z)}} \text{DET}$$

To deal with this, we first convert the premises to a sentence compatible to natural logic syntax, i.e., *quantifier x y*. Then we apply the above rules on these sentences to get inferences. Finally we convert sentences in natural logic to sentence in natural language. This usually only involves minimal editing. For example, *every* cat *(animal ∧ meow)* will be converted to "every cat is an animal who meows". As we will show later, DET is useful in solving many of the multi-premise problems in the first section of FraCaS. It is also worth noting that the capacity of our system can be easily expanded by including more rules from natural logic.

Initial knowledge base $\mathcal{K}$ includes the most basic (monotonicity) knowledge that can be utilized for all problems:

- **knowledge from WordNet** (Miller, 1995). dog $\leq$ animal, dog $|$ cat, etc. The first section of the FraCaS dataset does not require world knowledge, so we didn't include WordNet relations for now. However, they can easily be added if need be.

- **knowledge about quantifiers**. Our system treats the following words/phrases as quantifiers:
  - *every = all = each $\leq$ most $\leq$ many $\leq$ a few = several $\leq$ some = a; the $\leq$ some = a*
  - *at least/most n.*

  Because the parsers do not treat *at least/most n* as quantifiers as we hoped, we need a separate work-around for them.

---

[2]For example, s_1 = *a man walks*, s_2 = *no man walks*, s_3 = *some man walks*. We see that s_2 contradicts s_1 and that s_3 contradicts s_2, but s_3 is the same as s_1. This is also noted in Angeli et al. (2016).

system	MM08	AM14	LS13	T14	D14	M15	A16	ours
multi-premise?	N	N	Y	Y	Y	Y	Y	Y
# problems	44	44	74	74	74	74	74	74
Acc. (%)	97.73	95	62	80	95	77	93	88

Truth / Pred	E	U	C
Entail	29	7	0
Unknown	0	33	0
Contradict	0	2	3

Table 1: Left: Accuracy of our system and previous ones. Right: confusion matrix of our system. Our system achieves 100% precision and comparable accuracy with others. MM08: MacCartney and Manning (2008). AM14: Angeli and Manning (2014). LS13: Lewis and Steedman (2013). T14: Tian et al. (2014). D14: Dong et al. (2014). M15: Mineshima et al. (2015). A16: Abzianidze (2016).

3 Experiments on section 1 of FraCaS

We run our algorithm on the FraCaS dataset for NLI. This paper reports only on the first section: generalized quantifiers. Extending to other sections of the FraCaS dataset, and to other datasets, is work in progress. Results of our system are shown in Table 1. We have perfect precision and a comparable accuracy with previous systems.

3.1 Choice of parsers and their errors

Parser performance is the biggest bottle-neck of the system. We have tested two commonly used CCG parsers, C&C (Clark and Curran, 2007) and EasyCCG (Lewis and Steedman, 2014). C&C fails to parse four sentences from Sec. 1 of FraCaS. EasyCCG can parse all of them but we still need to semi-automatically modify the trees. Some of these are modifications that transform the tree into a semantically more meaningful form, while others are correcting parse errors. For example, not all quantifiers are super-tagged consistently, e.g., *most*, *few* are sometimes not tagged as NP/N. There are parsing errors involving multi-word expressions such as "a lot of", "used to be". We only correct systematic ones.

3.2 An example

The following example shows the actual process solving FraCas-026, which is a multiple-premise problem, and handled not only by replacement, but also with DET rule. Major steps are listed below:

1. Get polarities[3] of all premises $\mathcal{P}$, but not the hypothesis H:
   P1: Most$^\uparrow$ Europeans$^=$ are$^\uparrow$ resident$^\uparrow$ in$^\uparrow$ Europe$^\uparrow$
   P2: All$^\uparrow$ Europeans$^\downarrow$ are$^\uparrow$ people$^\uparrow$
   P3: All$^\uparrow$ people$^\downarrow$ who$^\downarrow$ are$^\downarrow$ resident$^\downarrow$ in$^\downarrow$ Europe$^\downarrow$ can$^\uparrow$ travel$^\uparrow$ freely$^\uparrow$ within$^\uparrow$ Europe$^\downarrow$
   H: Most Europeans can travel freely within Europe

2. Update knowledge base $\mathcal{K}$ with the information from $\mathcal{P}$, e.g.:
   Based on the form "every (or equivalent quantifiers, see above) X VP", add $X \leq VP$, which is:
   people who are resident in Europe $\leq$ can travel freely within Europe
   We can also get: *be people who are resident in Europe $\leq$ can travel freely within Europe*

3. Using the DET rule, the system generates a series of sentences which are also polarized, e.g., applying the DET rule to P1 and P2 we get:
   Most$^\uparrow$ Europeans$^=$ are$^\uparrow$ people$^\uparrow$ who$^\uparrow$ are$^\uparrow$ resident$^\uparrow$ in$^\uparrow$ Europe$^\uparrow$

4. Then adds generated sentences into sentence base $\mathcal{S}$, and start to do `replacement` on every constituent of each sentence. Therefore, we obtain a series of inferences like the following:
   Many European are people who are resident in Europe
   Most European are people
   Most European can travel freely within Europe
   Several European are people who are resitdent in Europe

---

[3]The polarity marking in P3 of the second occurrence of *Europe* was corrected from our system's output. The point is that under the scope of a modal *can*, a prepositional phrase headed by *in* or *within* changes polarity.

5. At last, one of the sentences in the list of inferences above matches the given hypothesis H, which means that solution to the original problem is `entail`.

4   Comparison with previous systems

We comment on our system and compare it to several systems mentioned in our Introduction (e.g. Mac-Cartney and Manning, 2008; Angeli and Manning, 2014; Mineshima et al., 2015; Abzianidze, 2015).

Our algorithm is *provably correct* in the following sense. If one has a correctly-parsed set $\mathcal{P} = P_1, \ldots, P_n$ of premises and uses our algorithm, and if the hypothesis H is proved from the premises in our system, then H follows logically from $\mathcal{P}$. So in this sense, our system will have no false positives, i.e., no type I error. Now this requires words of clarification. First, frequently the parsed output does not reflect the logical structure accurately, and in this case, the polarity-marking step of our algorithm might well go wrong. Second, in the case of ambiguous logical words, it is also possible that errors in a parse will lead to errors in our output. For example, the English word "any" means "all" in a downward-entailing environment, but it means "some" in an upward-entailing environment. There are exceptions to this.

MacCartney and Angeli's systems, on the other hand, find downward-entailing environments by pattern-matching using dependency trees, which makes the polarizing algorithm more error-prone. For example, their system (part of Stanford CoreNLP v3.9.1) incorrectly polarizes the following sentences: $no^\uparrow\ man^\downarrow\ walks^\uparrow$, $Ed^\uparrow\ refused^\uparrow\ to^\uparrow\ dance^\uparrow$, $John^\uparrow\ loves^\uparrow\ dancing^\uparrow\ without^\uparrow\ shoes^\uparrow$, $I^\uparrow\ like^\uparrow\ most^\uparrow\ dogs^\uparrow$, whereas our system correctly polarizes all of them (*walks*, *dance*, *shoes* should all be $\downarrow$ and *dogs* $=$). Another difference is that in our system, `replacement` can happen in any order, and the results are the same, whereas in Angeli's system only certain "mutating" orders lead to the correct inferences (see Section 3.1 of Angeli et al. (2016)). A final point is that their systems only polarize at the word level, but our system computes polarities also on the constituent level, which is important for `replacement` as shown in the example above.

We used the tool in Hu and Moss (2018), but they did not provide a working system for NLI. Such a system was described in Hu et al. (2018), but that paper was programmatic and did not have an implementation, or test data. So it left open the issue of how much NLI can be done with mononotonicity alone, and how much requires natural logic rules. We present initial attempts to address this problem.

The best-performing system in the logic-related area of NLI is the one described in Abzianidze (2014, 2015, 2017). That line of work uses tableau rules rather than deduction, as a more standard theorem-prover from automated reasoning. Our system is arguably simpler than his: we use no lambda logical forms, and we believe that the theoretical basis of our system is also simpler. When our system finds an inference (or contradiction) the derivations in our system are not so far from a natural language proof of the hypothesis (or its negation) from the premises. This would not be possible from a tableau proof.

5   Conclusion and future work

We have provided a generic algorithm for natural language inference based on polarized parses and natural logic rules. The algorithm requires parsed output, but it does not require translation into a logical form, or special alignment steps. It would be possible to extend our system in either or both directions.

For future work, we are currently tuning our system on other sections of the FraCaS dataset (especially Sections 5 and 6) and the larger SICK dataset (Marelli et al., 2014). Another line of work is to incorporate into our system some "light" representation of the sentences, e.g. dependency parses, abstract meaning representation, that allows for more flexible syntactic variation than the current string-for-string match strategy.

References

Abzianidze, L. (2014). Towards a wide-coverage tableau method for natural logic. In *New Frontiers in Artificial Intelligence - JSAI-isAI 2014 Workshops, LENLS, JURISIN, and GABA, Kanagawa, Japan, October 27-28, 2014, Revised Selected Papers*, pp. 66–82.

Abzianidze, L. (2015). A tableau prover for natural logic and language. In *Proceedings of the 2015 Conference on Empirical Methods in Natural Language Processing, EMNLP 2015, Lisbon, Portugal, September 17-21, 2015*, pp. 2492–2502.

Abzianidze, L. (2016). Natural solution to fracas entailment problems. In *Proceedings of the Fifth Joint Conference on Lexical and Computational Semantics*, pp. 64–74.

Abzianidze, L. (2017). Langpro: Natural language theorem prover. In *Proceedings of the 2017 Conference on Empirical Methods in Natural Language Processing: System Demonstrations*, pp. 115–120.

Angeli, G. and C. Manning (2014). NaturalLI: Natural logic inference for common sense reasoning. In *EMNLP*, pp. 534–545.

Angeli, G., N. Nayak, and C. Manning (2016). Combining natural logic and shallow reasoning for question answering. In *ACL*, pp. 442–452.

Bowman, S. R., C. Potts, and C. D. Manning (2015). Learning distributed word representations for natural logic reasoning. In *AAAI Spring Symposium on Knowledge Representation and Reasoning*, pp. 10–13.

Cases, I. and L. Karttunen (2017). Neural networks and textual inference: How did we get here and where do we go now?

Clark, S. and J. R. Curran (2007). Wide-coverage efficient statistical parsing with CCG and log-linear models. *Computational Linguistics 33*(4), 493–552.

Cooper, R., D. Crouch, J. Van Eijck, C. Fox, J. Van Genabith, J. Jaspars, H. Kamp, D. Milward, M. Pinkal, M. Poesio, et al. (1996). Using the framework. Technical report, Technical Report LRE 62-051 D-16, The FraCaS Consortium.

Dong, Y., R. Tian, and Y. Miyao (2014). Encoding generalized quantifiers in dependency-based compositional semantics. In *Proceedings of the 28th Pacific Asia Conference on Language, Information and Computing*.

Fyodorov, Y., Y. Winter, and N. Fyodorov (2003). Order-based inference in natural logic. *Log. J. IGPL 11*(4), 385–417. Inference in computational semantics: the Dagstuhl Workshop 2000.

Hu, H., T. F. Icard, and L. S. Moss (2018). Automated reasoning from polarized parse trees. In *Proceedings of the Fifth Workshop on Natural Language and Computer Science*.

Hu, H. and L. S. Moss (2018). Polarity computations in flexible categorial grammar. In *Proceedings of the Seventh Joint Conference on Lexical and Computational Semantics*, pp. 124–129.

Lewis, M. and M. Steedman (2013). Combined distributional and logical semantics. *Transactions of the Association of Computational Linguistics 1*, 179–192.

Lewis, M. and M. Steedman (2014). A* CCG parsing with a supertag-factored model. In *Proceedings of the 2014 Conference on Empirical Methods in Natural Language Processing (EMNLP)*, pp. 990–1000.

MacCartney, B. and C. D. Manning (2008). Modeling semantic containment and exclusion in natural language inference. In *Proceedings of COLING*, pp. 521–528. Association for Computational Linguistics.

MacCartney, B. and C. D. Manning (2009). An extended model of natural logic. In *IWCS-8, Proceedings of the Eighth International Conference on Computational Semantics*, pp. 140–156.

Marelli, M., S. Menini, M. Baroni, L. Bentivogli, R. Bernardi, and R. Zamparelli (2014). A SICK cure for the evaluation of compositional distributional semantic models.

Miller, G. A. (1995). Wordnet: a lexical database for English. *Communications of the ACM 38*(11), 39–41.

Mineshima, K., P. Martínez-Gómez, Y. Miyao, and D. Bekki (2015). Higher-order logical inference with compositional semantics. In *Proceedings of the 2015 Conference on Empirical Methods in Natural Language Processing*, pp. 2055–2061.

Tian, R., Y. Miyao, and T. Matsuzaki (2014). Logical inference on dependency-based compositional semantics. In *Proceedings of the 52nd Annual Meeting of the Association for Computational Linguistics (Volume 1: Long Papers)*, Volume 1, pp. 79–89.

van Benthem, J. (1986). *Essays in Logical Semantics*, Volume 29 of *Studies in Linguistics and Philosophy*. Dordrecht: D. Reidel Publishing Co.

Zamansky, A., N. Francez, and Y. Winter (2006). A 'natural logic' inference system using the Lambek calculus. *Journal of Logic, Language, and Information 15*(3), 273–295.

A   Pseudocode of our system

Algorithm 1 Infer with Monotonicity

1: **procedure** MYPROCEDURE(*premises*, H)
2: build s and k:
3: $s \leftarrow$ *SentenceBase*() ▷ initialize s
4: $k \leftarrow$ *KnowledgeBase*() ▷ initialize k
5: k.*buildQuantifier*() ▷ add to k: all = every = each $\leq$ some = a
6: k.*buildMorphTense*() ▷ add to k: man = men, have = has
7: **for** P in *premises* **do**
8:   P.*fixTree*()
9:   k.*extractPattern*(P) ▷ add to k: "every x is NP" $\rightarrow$ $x \leq NP$
10:   k.*updateWordLists*(P) ▷ add to k: all nouns, adjs, rel clauses, etc. in P
11:   s.*addInference*(P) ▷ add to s: P
12: **end for**
13: k.*updateWordLists*(H) ▷ add to k: all nouns, adjs, rel clauses, etc. in H
14: s.*addHypothesis*(H) ▷ add to s: H, "there be N who VP" $\rightarrow$ "some N VP"
15: update k:
16: k.*update*() ▷ adj + noun $\leq$ noun, noun + RC/PP $\leq$ noun, verb + PP $\leq$ verb
17: k.*updateRules*() ▷ SOME, ANTI, DET rules
18: polarize premises:
19: **for** P in *premises* **do**
20:   P.*polarize*()
21: **end for**
22: infer by replacement:
23: *infer*($s, k, depth$) ▷ depth = how many rounds of replacement; iterative deepening search
24: predict:
25: **if** H in s.inferences **then return** entail
26: **else**
27:   **if** H in s.contradictions **then return** contradiction
28:   **else return** unknown
29:   **end if**
30: **end if**
31: **end procedure**

Distributional semantics in the real world: building word vector representations from a truth-theoretic model

Elizaveta Kuzmenko & Aurélie Herbelot
University of Trento
{firstname}.{lastname}@unitn.it

Abstract

Distributional semantics models (DSMs) are known to produce excellent representations of word meaning, which correlate with a range of behavioural data. As lexical representations, they have been said to be fundamentally different from truth-theoretic models of semantics, where meaning is defined as a correspondence relation to the world. There are two main aspects to this difference: a) DSMs are built over corpus data which may or may not reflect 'what is in the world'; b) they are built from word co-occurrences, that is, from lexical types rather than entities and sets. In this paper, we inspect the properties of a distributional model built over a set-theoretic approximation of 'the real world'. To achieve this, we take the annotation a large database of images marked with objects, attributes and relations, convert the data into a representation akin to first-order logic and build several distributional models using various combinations of features. We evaluate those models over both relatedness and similarity datasets, demonstrating their effectiveness in standard evaluations. This allows us to conclude that, despite prior claims, truth-theoretic models are good candidates for building graded lexical representations of meaning.

1 Introduction

In recent years, distributional semantics models (DSMs) (Erk, 2012; Clark, 2012; Turney and Pantel, 2010) have received close attention from the linguistic community. One reason for this is that they are known to produce excellent representations of lexical meaning, which account for similarity and polysemy and correlate well with a range of behavioural data (Lenci, 2008; Mandera et al., 2017). DSMs are built on the basis of word co-occurrences in large corpora, stemming from the hypothesis that words co-occurring in similar contexts tend to share their meaning (Firth, 1957). As such, they are fundamentally different from truth-theoretic models of semantics, where meaning is defined as a correspondence relation between predicates and the world. This difference can be explicated further by noting two features of DSMs. First, they are built over corpus data which may or may not reflect 'what is in the world' (Herbelot, 2013) – and consequently does not reflect human experience gained from real world data (Andrews et al., 2009). Second, they are built from *word* co-occurrences, that is, from lexical types rather than entities and sets. In contrast, formal models account for denotation and set-theoretic aspects of language, but they are often said to lack the ability to account for lexical similarity and gradedness. This has been the basis for wanting to combine formal and distributional semantics in the past (Boleda and Herbelot, 2016): the role of DSMs, it is claimed, is to bring the lexicon to denotational approaches to meaning.

In the present paper, we build a large set-theoretic model as an approximation of "the real world", and show that quality vector representations can in fact be extracted from it. To obtain our model, we take the annotation of the Visual Genome (henceforth VG), a large database of images annotated with objects, attributes and relations (Krishna et al., 2017), and regard this data as an informative, although incomplete, description of the world. We convert the annotated data into a representation akin to some underspecified first-order logic. From this representation, we build several DSMs from various aspects of the representation and inspect the properties of the created spaces. We evaluate our models with both relatedness and similarity datasets (MEN, Bruni et al., 2012, and SimLex-999, Hill et al., 2015).

2   Related Work

Our work fits into attempts to bridge the gap between distributional and formal semantics. The subfield of Formal Distributional Semantics (FDS, Boleda and Herbelot, 2016) includes efforts to a) investigate the mapping from distributional models to formal semantic models (Herbelot and Vecchi, 2015; Erk, 2016; Wang et al., 2017); b) enrich formal semantics with distributional data (Garrette et al., 2011; Beltagy et al., 2013); and c) account for particular logical phenomena in vector spaces, including composition (Coecke et al., 2011; Boleda et al., 2013; Baroni et al., 2012; Bernardi et al., 2013; Asher et al., 2016 amongst many others). We also note the relevance of the work on constructing distributional spaces from syntactically or semantically parsed data (e.g. Padó and Lapata, 2007; Grefenstette et al., 2014; Hermann and Blunsom, 2013), which echoes the way we construct vector spaces from various types of predicative contexts. In contrast to those efforts, however, our data is not a standard corpus reflecting word usage but a collection of logical forms expressing true sentences with respect to a model of the world.

Most similar to our endeavour is the work by Young et al. (2014), who also take multimodal datasets as a basis to learn denotations. Their model is however created for the task of semantic inference and takes the extension of a word to be the set of situations it applies to. We introduce notions of entities and properties in our own model.

3   Building a truth-theoretic space

In order to build a "real world" space, we require a representation akin to a set-theoretic model. We take the annotation of the Visual Genome (VG) dataset (Krishna et al., 2017) as a proxy for such model, under the assumption that it provides a set of 'true' sentences about the world. VG contains 108,077 images associated with structured annotations. There are three types of annotation in the dataset: a) entities, or **objects** (e.g. *'window'*, *'elephant'*) – the individuals present in a given image; b) **attributes** (e.g. *'red'*, *'made of bricks'*) which describe the properties of objects; c) **relationships** (e.g. *'on'*, *'has'*, *'wearing'*) which correspond to relations between objects. The dataset also features situations, or **scene graphs**, which correspond to a single image and describe all the objects that co-occur in that image. Thus, a situation might contain a tree, a car, a woman, a dog, a sidewalk and a shade (from the tree), associated with bounding boxes. We do not use the image itself but solely the annotation data from the graph.

Every object in VG is assigned a WordNet synset and a unique id. This allows us to pre-process the data into shallow logical forms corresponding to predicate / entity pairs, ordered by situation and implicitly coordinated by a $\wedge$ within that situation. For instance, the following toy example indicates that situation 1 contains a tall brick building, identified by variable 1058505 in VG, on which we find a black sign, identified by variable 1058507. Note that the identifiers are 'real-world' variables, which pick out particular objects in the world.

$$S1 \quad building.n.01(1058508), tall(1058508), brick(1058508)$$
$$sign.n.02(1058507), black(1058507), on(1058507,1058508)$$

Intuitively, this representation allows us to capture all the distinct objects annotated with e.g. the synset *'building.n.01'* to generate the set of buildings ($building'$) in our universe.[1] To avoid data sparsity, we convert all relations into one-place predicates, by replacing each argument in turn with its corresponding synset. So in the example above, $on(1058507,1058508)$ becomes $on(1058507,building.n.01)$, $on(sign.n.02,1058508)$, which formalises that 1058507 is in the set of things that are on buildings, while 1058508 is in the set of things that signs are on.

Formally, the VG data can then be considered a set-theoretic model $M = < U,I >$ where U is the universe (the set of all objects in the model, as identified by 'real-world' variables), and I is an interpretation function mapping from a set of n-place predicates P to n-tuples of objects in U (with $n = 1$ given our pre-processing of relations). P is the union of synsets (Syn), attributes (Att) and

---

[1]Note that we are not making use of the sense information provided by the synset in this work. Most words in VG are anyway used in a unique sense.

relations (*Rel*) in VG. We then build a distributional space $S = <U,P,D,F,A,C>$ where U and P are the universe and the predicates as above; D are the dimensions of the space so that $D \subseteq P$ (that is, any combination of *Syn*, *Att* and *Rel*); and F some extraction function over our corpus of shallow logical forms C. F is of the form $U \times D \rightarrow \{0,1\}$, i.e. it returns whether a particular dimension is predicated of an entity, giving us boolean entity vectors for all objects in VG. Finally, an aggregation function $A : (U \times D \rightarrow \{0,1\}) \rightarrow (P \times D \rightarrow \mathbb{N}_0)$ returns the final space by summing the entity vectors corresponding to each predicate in P: $\mathbb{N}_0$ is a natural number expressing how many times dimension D is predicated of entities of type P. The summing operation follows the model-theoretic intuition that a predicate p denotes a set which is the *union* of all things that are p: for instance, all dog entity vectors are summed to produce a vector for the predicate dog′.

In addition, we consider two ways to augment this original setup. One is by adding situational information to the mix: while relations give us a handle on what type of things a particular entity associates with via a particular predicate, this information does not include the type of things the entity simply *co-occurs* with. For instance, we may have a situation where a dog interacts with a ball (encoded by some relation *dog - chew - ball*), but VG relations do not directly tell us that the dog entity co-occurs with a park entity or a cloud entity. Another way to augment the data is by adding encyclopedic information to the VG data, which could be part of a more 'complete' model including some generalizations over the encoded sets. To do this, we extract hypernyms from WordNet (Miller et al., 1990) using the *nltk* package.[2] Only one level – the immediate parents of the concept – is taken into account. We note that hypernyms are different from the other VG features in that they don't come from natural utterances (no one would say *"domestic animal"* in place of *"dog"* in a natural context).

In what follows, we build variations of the model M by counting co-occurrences between our basic entity set (aggregated into predicates with function A) and the following features $D \subseteq P$: attributes (*Att*), relations (*Rel*), situations (*Sit*), hypernyms (*Hyp*), and all combinations thereof.[3]

4   Evaluation

To measure the quality of constructed models, we evaluate them on two standard datasets: MEN and SimLex-999. The MEN dataset is supposed to capture the relatedness notion, which is defined as the relation between pairs of entities that are associated but not actually similar. SimLex-999 accounts for similarity, which is defined as the relation between words which share physical or functional features, as well as categorical information (Hill et al., 2015). Both datasets are structured in the same way: they consist of word pairs human-coded for their level of association. They respectively include 3000 (MEN) and 999 (SimLex) word pairs. To evaluate our DSMs, we follow standard practice and compute the Spearman ρ correlation between the cosine similarity scores given by the model and the gold annotation. Results are shown in Table 1. To maximise comparability between different spaces and with text corpora, scores are given for raw co-occurrence matrices, and no dimensionality reduction or other optimization of the space is conducted. Note that due to the size of VG, we cannot evaluate on all pairs in the datasets. We show actual coverage in brackets next to the correlation scores.

Trends are similar both for MEN and SimLex-999. We get overall best results (highlighted in **bold**) for the models built using relations, situational information, and relations together with situations. Other models have significantly lower quality, both for single features and for their combinations. It should be noted that taking all the features together does not improve the quality of the space.

In the last column of Table 1 we report the total number of co-occurrences in each variation of the world-based model. They are included in order to make sure that we do not observe solely the effect of increasing the amount of data. Indeed, models with the greatest number of co-occurrences show medium quality, and for some combinations of features the score even decreases with more data (e.g., compare the *Hyp* and *Hyp + Sit* models, where the MEN score stays more or less the same and the SimLex score

---

[2] http://www.nltk.org/

[3] The code to pre-process the Visual Genome and the data to reproduce the experiments can be found at https://github.com/lizaku/dsm-from-vg.

Setting	MEN	SimLex-999	Num. co-occurrences
Attributes (*Att*)	0.1801 (871)	0.1119 (217)	1 854 033
Relations (*Rel*)	**0.5499** (847)	**0.2861** (216)	6 481 872
Situations (*Sit*)	**0.5294** (847)	**0.2480** (216)	22 894 730
Hypernyms (*Hyp*)	0.3399 (956)	0.2128 (244)	1 989 576
Att + Rel	0.346 (871)	0.1840 (217)	10 720 260
Att + Sit	0.4492 (871)	0.2042 (217)	25 988 265
Rel + Sit	**0.5326** (847)	**0.2463** (216)	32 170 563
Att + Hyp	0.2385 (975)	0.2055 (244)	5 114 997
Rel + Hyp	**0.5193** (956)	**0.2979** (244)	10 878 274
Hyp + Sit	0.3860 (956)	0.1731 (244)	26 882 218
Att + Rel + Hyp	0.3430 (975)	0.2367 (244)	16 391 743
Att + Rel + Sit	0.4503 (871)	0.2018 (217)	37 652 176
Att + Sit + Hyp	0.3260 (975)	0.1319 (244)	31 252 206
Rel + Hyp + Sit	0.3900 (956)	0.1760 (244)	38 571 325
Att + Rel + Hyp + Sit	0.3283 (975)	0.1337 (244)	45 329 361

Table 1: Spearman ρ correlation for various models on MEN and SimLex-999.

Count-based		Predictive (word2vec)		Co-occurrences
MEN	SimLex-999	MEN	SimLex-999	
0.081 (749)	0.050 (462)	0.024 (749)	0.003 (462)	2 000 000
0.158 (995)	0.010 (546)	0.043 (995)	0.019 (546)	5 000 000
0.225 (1226)	0.038 (610)	0.049 (1226)	0.020 (610)	15 000 000
0.226 (1455)	0.037 (688)	0.031 (1455)	0.046 (688)	30 000 000
0.253 (1554)	0.056 (696)	0.031 (1554)	0.044 (696)	40 000 000

Table 2: Spearman correlation on MEN and SimLex-999 datasets (Wikipedia spaces)

becomes lower). Moreover, the *Rel* model shows the highest score on a moderately small amount of data for the MEN dataset, and for the SimLex-999 dataset the score is a bit lower, whereas the *Rel + Hyp* model becomes the best (though hypernyms come from outside the model).

To compare performance of our truth-theoretic models with traditional DSMs built from text corpora, we create count-based models from the English Wikipedia using a window of $\pm$ 2 words around a target. We modulate corpus size to roughly match the number of co-occurrences extracted from VG.[4] Additionally, we train predictive models with Word2Vec (Mikolov et al., 2013) with the same number of co-occurrences as in the count-based variants. We use the same window size of 2, and the dimensionality of vectors is set to 300. The evaluation scores for different corpora sizes are shown in Table 2. We can see that, in contrast with the VG models, the score for count-based models is dependent on the amount of data provided to the DSM, and generally lower for similar numbers of co-occurrences (scores are consistent with results reported by Sahlgren and Lenci, 2016). Predictive models are simply not able to construct high-quality word representations from such amount of data.

When we try to improve the quality of our best world-based model (*Rel*) by applying normalisation, dimensionality reduction (to 300 dimensions) and PPMI weighting, we reach scores of **0.6539** on MEN (847 pairs are evaluated because not all of the pairs in the evaluation dataset are present in the VG space) and **0.3353** on SimLex-999 (216 pairs evaluated). Whilst results are not directly comparable, we nevertheless note that the MEN score is close to the figure of 0.68 reported for the inter-annotator

---

[4]Models are built using `https://github.com/akb89/entropix`

correlation on the full 3000 pairs.[5] It is also only a few points lower than the best score of 0.72 obtained by Baroni et al. (2014) over 2.6B words (around 1600 times more data than in *Rel* on the basis of a ± 2 word window size). The SimLex figure is also well above the figure of 0.233 reported by Hill et al. (2015) on an SVD model trained over 150M words ($\approx$ 100 times more data).

5   Discussion

Some interesting observations can be made with regard to the type of properties that seem to be relevant to modeling conceptual association. First, the relative results we are observing across the VG models are not artefactual of model size. Thus, a model based on situations, with 22M co-occurrences, performs worse than the model with relations, which comprises only 6M co-occurrences. This tells us that some aspects of the model-theoretic data are much more important than others and that some can even be detrimental. This finding echoes results in Emerson and Copestake (2016), which indicated that selecting particular relations from parsed data can improve performance on SimLex.

Second, the VG models outperform the standard spaces by a large margin on SimLex, even with small amounts of data. This confirms that SimLex encodes a notion of similarity that is better captured by looking at how things 'are' truth-theoretically rather than what we say about them. The fact that attributes perform badly on that dataset, however, contradicts the idea that SimLex encodes similarity of intrinsic features. Indeed, *relations* outperform any other combination of features, showing that how things associate with other things may be more important than how they intrinsically are.

Third, an additional point can be made about relations and situations. While both *Rel* and *Sit* models perform well on their own, the combined *Rel + Sit* model has lower quality (around two points are lost on MEN and four points on SimLex, compared to *Rel* alone), which means that situations take the score down. This can be explained by the fact that situations are a "noisy superset" of relations: some of the entities that co-occur in a situation will have an explicit relation associated with them (e.g., *cat* and *mouse* related by *chase'(x,y)*), while others may indeed solely co-occur (e.g., *cat* and *fork* in a scene with a pet sitting next to a dining table). So it seems that aspects of the world that entities are *actively* involved in are more important to define them than simple 'bystander' individuals.

Finally, using hypernyms improves the quality of models when evaluated on SimLex. This confirms previous results showing that using dictionaries and lexical databases helps getting better performance on SimLex (Faruqui and Dyer, 2015; Recski et al., 2016). It also indicates than when computing similarity, humans may indeed activate some 'meta-knowledge' which is not directly encoded in the basic level categories (Rosch et al., 1976) people use to describe a situation.

6   Conclusion

Both distributional semantics and formal semantics have their own advantages and disadvantages, but their unification provides a really powerful tool for studying the interaction between similarity and relatedness, as well as finding out which properties human tap into when making association judgments.

This paper has shown that we can study the distributional behaviour of concepts from a (large enough) truth-theoretic model. Thus, standard distributional semantics is not unique in accounting for conceptual distance. Further, the vector spaces we created have the advantages of formal models, by linking to a clear notion of entity and associated properties. Crucially, we have also demonstrated that by choosing the right properties, the truth-theoretic vector space achieves superior performance compared to a usage-based DSM on considerably less data. While this point does not have practical application, we believe this result may have implications for understanding how humans themselves build concepts from the limited set of situations they are exposed to.

In the future, we will experiment with other image-annotated datasets or knowledge graphs to further understand which formal relations might be at the basis of human similarity judgments.

---

[5]See `https://staff.fnwi.uva.nl/e.bruni/MEN`.

References

Andrews, M., G. Vigliocco, and D. Vinson (2009). Integrating experiential and distributional data to learn semantic representations. *Psychological review 116*(3), 463.

Asher, N., T. Van de Cruys, A. Bride, and M. Abrusán (2016). Integrating type theory and distributional semantics: a case study on adjective–noun compositions. *Computational Linguistics 42*(4), 703–725.

Baroni, M., R. Bernardi, N.-Q. Do, and C.-c. Shan (2012). Entailment above the word level in distributional semantics. In *Proceedings of the 13th Conference of the European Chapter of the Association for Computational Linguistics*, pp. 23–32. Association for Computational Linguistics.

Baroni, M., G. Dinu, and G. Kruszewski (2014). Don't count, predict! a systematic comparison of context-counting vs. context-predicting semantic vectors. In *ACL (1)*, pp. 238–247.

Beltagy, I., C. Chau, G. Boleda, D. Garrette, K. Erk, and R. Mooney (2013). Montague meets markov: Deep semantics with probabilistic logical form. In *Second Joint Conference on Lexical and Computational Semantics (*SEM2013)*, Atlanta, Georgia, USA, pp. 11–21.

Bernardi, R., G. Dinu, M. Marelli, and M. Baroni (2013). A relatedness benchmark to test the role of determiners in compositional distributional semantics. In *Proceedings of the 51st Annual Meeting of the Association for Computational Linguistics (Volume 2: Short Papers)*, Volume 2, pp. 53–57.

Boleda, G., M. Baroni, T. N. Pham, and L. McNally (2013). Intensionality was only alleged: On adjective-noun composition in distributional semantics. In *Proceedings of the 10th International Conference on Computational Semantics (IWCS2013)*, Potsdam, Germany, pp. 35–46.

Boleda, G. and A. Herbelot (2016). Formal distributional semantics: Introduction to the special issue. *Computational Linguistics 42*(4), 619–635.

Bruni, E., G. Boleda, M. Baroni, and N.-K. Tran (2012). Distributional semantics in technicolor. In *Proceedings of the 50th Annual Meeting of the Association for Computational Linguistics: Long Papers-Volume 1*, pp. 136–145. Association for Computational Linguistics.

Clark, S. (2012). Vector space models of lexical meaning. In S. Lappin and C. Fox (Eds.), *Handbook of Contemporary Semantics – second edition*. Wiley-Blackwell.

Coecke, B., M. Sadrzadeh, and S. Clark (2011). Mathematical foundations for a compositional distributional model of meaning. *Linguistic Analysis: A Festschrift for Joachim Lambek 36*(1–4), 345–384.

Emerson, G. and A. Copestake (2016). Functional distributional semantics. *arXiv preprint arXiv:1606.08003*.

Erk, K. (2012). Vector space models of word meaning and phrase meaning: a survey. *Language and Linguistics Compass 6*, 635–653.

Erk, K. (2016). What do you know about an alligator when you know the company it keeps? *Semantics and Pragmatics 9*, 17–1.

Faruqui, M. and C. Dyer (2015). Non-distributional word vector representations. In *Proceedings of the 53rd Annual Meeting of the Association for Computational Linguistics and the 7th International Joint Conference on Natural Language Processing (ACL2015)*, Volume 2, pp. 464–469.

Firth, J. R. (1957). A synopsis of linguistic theory, 1930-1955. studies in linguistic analysis. *Oxford: Philological Society. [Reprinted in Selected Papers of J.R. Firth 1952-1959, ed. Frank R. Palmer, 1968. London: Longman]*.

Garrette, D., K. Erk, and R. Mooney (2011). Integrating logical representations with probabilistic information using Markov logic. In *Proceedings of the Ninth International Conference on Computational Semantics (IWCS2011)*, pp. 105–114.

Grefenstette, E., M. Sadrzadeh, S. Clark, B. Coecke, and S. Pulman (2014). Concrete sentence spaces for compositional distributional models of meaning. In *Computing meaning*, pp. 71–86. Springer.

Herbelot, A. (2013). What is in a text, what isn't, and what this has to do with lexical semantics. In *Proceedings of the Tenth International Conference on Computational Semantics (IWCS 2013)*, Potsdam, Germany.

Herbelot, A. and E. M. Vecchi (2015). Building a shared world: Mapping distributional to model-theoretic semantic spaces. In *Proceedings of the 2015 Conference on Empirical Methods in Natural Language Processing*, pp. 22–32.

Hermann, K. M. and P. Blunsom (2013). The role of syntax in vector space models of compositional semantics. In *Proceedings of the 51st Annual Meeting of the Association for Computational Linguistics (Volume 1: Long Papers)*, Volume 1, pp. 894–904.

Hill, F., R. Reichart, and A. Korhonen (2015). Simlex-999: Evaluating semantic models with (genuine) similarity estimation. *Computational Linguistics 41*(4), 665–695.

Krishna, R., Y. Zhu, O. Groth, J. Johnson, K. Hata, J. Kravitz, S. Chen, Y. Kalantidis, L.-J. Li, D. A. Shamma, et al. (2017). Visual genome: Connecting language and vision using crowdsourced dense image annotations. *International Journal of Computer Vision 123*(1), 32–73.

Lenci, A. (2008). Distributional semantics in linguistic and cognitive research. *Italian journal of linguistics 20*(1), 1–31.

Mandera, P., E. Keuleers, and M. Brysbaert (2017). Explaining human performance in psycholinguistic tasks with models of semantic similarity based on prediction and counting: A review and empirical validation. *Journal of Memory and Language 92*, 57–78.

Mikolov, T., W.-t. Yih, and G. Zweig (2013). Linguistic regularities in continuous space word representations. In *HLT-NAACL*, pp. 746–751.

Miller, G. A., R. Beckwith, C. Fellbaum, D. Gross, and K. J. Miller (1990). Introduction to wordnet: An on-line lexical database. *International journal of lexicography 3*(4), 235–244.

Padó, S. and M. Lapata (2007). Dependency-Based Construction of Semantic Space Models. *Computational Linguistics 33*(2), 161–199.

Recski, G., E. Iklódi, K. Pajkossy, and A. Kornai (2016). Measuring semantic similarity of words using concept networks. In *Proceedings of the 1st Workshop on Representation Learning for NLP*, pp. 193–200.

Rosch, E., C. B. Mervis, W. D. Gray, D. M. Johnson, and P. Boyes-Braem (1976). Basic objects in natural categories. *Cognitive psychology 8*(3), 382–439.

Sahlgren, M. and A. Lenci (2016). The effects of data size and frequency range on distributional semantic models. In *Proceedings of the 2016 Conference on Empirical Methods in Natural Language Processing*, pp. 975–980.

Turney, P. D. and P. Pantel (2010). From frequency to meaning: Vector space models of semantics. *Journal of Artificial Intelligence Research 37*, 141–188.

Wang, S., S. Roller, and K. Erk (2017). Distributional modeling on a dict: One-shot word learning from text only. In *Proceedings of the Eighth International Joint Conference on Natural Language Processing*, Volume 1, pp. 204–213.

Young, P., A. Lai, M. Hodosh, and J. Hockenmaier (2014). From image descriptions to visual denotations: New similarity metrics for semantic inference over event descriptions. *Transactions of the Association for Computational Linguistics 2*, 67–78.

Linguistic Information in Neural Semantic Parsing
with Multiple Encoders

Rik van Noord   Antonio Toral   Johan Bos
Center for Language and Cognition, University of Groningen
{r.i.k.van.noord, a.toral.ruiz, johan.bos}@rug.nl

Abstract

Recently, sequence-to-sequence models have achieved impressive performance on a number of semantic parsing tasks. However, they often do not exploit available linguistic resources, while these, when employed correctly, are likely to increase performance even further. Research in neural machine translation has shown that employing this information has a lot of potential, especially when using a multi-encoder setup. We employ a range of semantic and syntactic resources to improve performance for the task of Discourse Representation Structure Parsing. We show that (i) linguistic features can be beneficial for neural semantic parsing and (ii) the best method of adding these features is by using multiple encoders.

1   Introduction

Sequence-to-sequence neural networks have shown remarkable performance in semantic parsing (Ling et al., 2016; Jia and Liang, 2016; Konstas et al., 2017; Dong and Lapata, 2018; Liu et al., 2018; Van Noord, Abzianidze, Toral, and Bos, 2018). This architecture is able to learn meaning representations for a range of semantic phenomena, usually without resorting to any linguistic information such as part-of-speech or syntax. Though this is an impressive feat in itself, there is no reason to abandon these resources. Even in machine translation, where models can be trained on relatively large data sets, it has been shown that sequence-to-sequence models can benefit from external syntactic and semantic resources (Sennrich and Haddow, 2016; Aharoni and Goldberg, 2017) and a multi-source approach has proved particularly successful for adding syntax (Currey and Heafield, 2018). The current approaches in neural semantic parsing either include (some) linguistic information in a single encoder (POS-tags in Van Noord and Bos 2017a,b, lemmas in Liu et al. 2018), or use multiple encoders to represent multiple languages rather than linguistic knowledge (Duong et al., 2017; Susanto and Lu, 2017). To our knowledge, we are the first to investigate the potential of exploiting linguistic information in a multi-encoder setup for (neural) semantic parsing.

Specifically, the aims of this paper are to investigate (i) whether exploiting linguistic information can improve semantic parsing and (ii) whether it is better to include this linguistic information in the same encoder or in an additional one. We take as baseline the neural semantic parser for Discourse Representation Structures (DRS, Kamp and Reyle, 1993; Van Noord, Abzianidze, Haagsma, and Bos, 2018) developed by Van Noord, Abzianidze, Toral, and Bos (2018). During encoding we add linguistic information in a multi-encoder setup, including various wide-spread automatic linguistic analyses for the input texts, ranging from lemmatisation, POS-tagging, syntactic analysis, to semantic tagging. We then empirically determine whether using a multi-encoder setup is preferable over merging all input features in a single encoder. The insight gained from these experiments will provide suggestions to improve future neural semantic parsing for DRSs and other semantic formalisms.

2 Data and Methodology

2.1 Discourse Representation Structures

DRSs are formal meaning representations based on Discourse Representation Theory (Kamp and Reyle, 1993). We use the version of DRT as provided in the Parallel Meaning Bank (PMB, Abzianidze et al. 2017), a semantically annotated parallel corpus, with texts in English, Italian, German and Dutch. DRSs are rich meaning representations containing quantification, negation, reference resolution, comparison operators, discourse relations, concepts based on WordNet, and semantic roles based on VerbNet.

All experiments are performed using the data of the PMB. In our experiments, we only use the English texts and corresponding DRSs. We use PMB release 2.2.0, which contains gold standard (fully manually annotated) data of which we use 4,597 as train, 682 as dev and 650 as test instances. It also contains 67,965 silver (partially manually annotated) and 120,662 bronze (no manual annotations) instances. Most sentences are between 5 and 15 tokens in length. Since we will compare our results mainly to Van Noord, Abzianidze, Toral, and Bos (2018), we will only employ the gold and silver data.

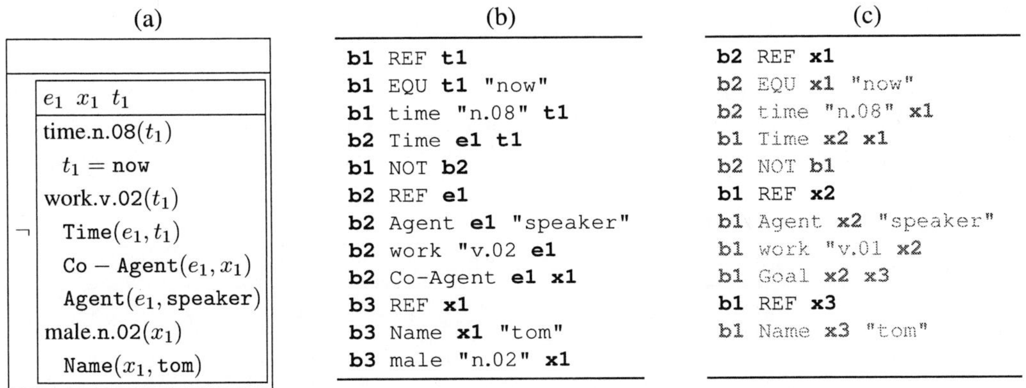

Figure 1: DRS in box format (a), gold clause representation (b) and example system output (c) for *I am not working for Tom*, with precision of 5/8 and recall of 5/9, resulting in an F-score of 58.8.

2.2 Representing Input and Output

We represent the source and target data in the same way as Van Noord, Abzianidze, Toral, and Bos (2018), who represent the source sentence as a sequence of characters, with a special character indicating uppercase characters. The target DRS is also represented as a sequence of characters, with the exception of DRS operators, thematic roles and DRS variables, which are represented as *super characters* (Van Noord and Bos, 2017b), i.e. individual tokens. Since the variable names itself are meaningless, the DRS variables are rewritten to a more general representation, using the De Bruijn index (de Bruijn, 1972). In a post-processing step, the original clause structured is restored.[1]

To include morphological and syntactic information, we apply a lemmatizer, POS-tagger and dependency parser using Stanford CoreNLP (Manning et al., 2014), similar to Sennrich and Haddow (2016) for machine translation. The lemmas and POS-tags are added as a token after each word. For the dependency parse, we add the incoming arc for each word. We also apply the easyCCG parser of Lewis and Steedman (2014), using the supertags.[2] Finally, we exploit semantic information by using semantic tags (Bjerva et al., 2016; Abzianidze and Bos, 2017). Semantic tags are language-neutral semantic categories, which get assigned to a word in a similar fashion as part-of-speech tags. Semantic tags are able to express important semantic distinctions, such as negation, modals and types of quantification. We train a semantic tagger with the TnT tagger (Brants, 2000) on the gold and silver standard data in the PMB release. Examples of the input to the model for each source of information are shown in Table 1.

---

[1] See Van Noord, Abzianidze, Toral, and Bos (2018) for a more detailed overview of the representation used.

[2] We segment the supertags, e.g. *(S\NP)\(S\NP)* is represented as *(S \ NP) \ (S \ NP)*

Table 1: Example representations for each source of input information.

Source	Representation
Sentence	I am not working for Tom .
Lemma	I be not work for Tom .
POS-tags	PRP VBP RB VBG IN NNP .
Dependency parse	nsubj aux neg ROOT case nmod punct
Semantic tags	PRO NOW NOT EXG REL PER NIL
CCG supertags	NP (S[dcl]\NP)/(S[ng]\NP) (S\NP)\(S\NP) (S[ng]\NP)/PP PP/NP N .

There are two ways to add the linguistic information; (1) merging all the information (i.e., input text and linguistic information) in a single encoder, or (2) using multiple encoders (i.e., encoding separately the input text and the linguistic information). Multi-source encoders were initially introduced for multilingual translation (Zoph and Knight, 2016; Firat et al., 2016; Libovický and Helcl, 2017), but recently were used to introduce syntactic information to the model (Currey and Heafield, 2018). Table 2 shows examples of how the input is structured for using one or more encoders.

Table 2: Example representation when using one or two encoders, for either a single source of information (POS) or multiple sources (POS + Sem) for the sentence *I am not working for Tom.* For readability purposes we show the word-level instead of character-level representation of the source words here.

Source	Encoder	Representation
POS - 1 enc	Enc 1	I PRP am VBP not RB working VBG for IN Tom NNP . .
POS - 2 enc	Enc 1	I am not working for Tom .
	Enc 2	PRP VBP RB VBG IN NNP .
POS + Sem - 1 enc	Enc 1	I PRP PRO am VBP NOW not RB NOT working VBG EXG for IN REL Tom NNP PER . . NIL
POS + Sem - 2 enc	Enc 1	I am not working for Tom .
	Enc 2	PRP PRO VBP NOW RB NOT VBG EXG IN REL NNP PER . NIL

Experiments showed that using more than two encoders drastically decreased performance. Therefore, we merge all the linguistic information in a single encoder (see last row of Table 2).

2.3 Neural Architecture

We employ a recurrent sequence-to-sequence neural network with attention (Bahdanau et al., 2014) and two bi-LSTM layers, similar to the one used by Van Noord, Abzianidze, Toral, and Bos (2018). However, their model was trained with *OpenNMT* (Klein et al., 2017), which does not support multiple encoders. Therefore, we switch to the sequence-to-sequence framework implemented in *Marian* (Junczys-Dowmunt et al., 2018). We use model-type *s2s* (for a single encoder) or *multi-s2s* (for multiple encoders).

For the latter, this means that the multiple inputs are encoded separately by an identical RNN (without sharing parameters). The encoders share a single decoder, in which the resulting context vectors are concatenated. An attention layer[3] is then applied to selectively give more attention to certain parts of the vector (i.e. it can learn that the words themselves are more important than just the POS-tags). A detailed overview of our parameter settings, found after a search on the dev set, can be found in Table 3. When only using gold data, training is stopped after 15 epochs. For gold + silver data, we stop training after 6 epochs, after which we restart the training process from that checkpoint to finetune on only the gold data, also for 6 epochs.

---

[3]This attention layer is the same for the single source setting.

Table 3: Parameter settings for the Marian seq2seq model, found after a search on the development set. Settings not mentioned are left at default.

Parameter	Value	Parameter	Value	Parameter	Value	Parameter	Value
RNN type	LSTM	Dropout RNN	0.2	Learning rate (LR)	0.002	Beam size	10
Enc type	bi-direc	Dropout src/tgt	0.0	LR decay	0.8	Length normalization	0.9
Enc/dec layers	2	Batch size	12	LR decay strategy	epoch	Label smoothing	0.1
Embedding size	300	Optimization crit	ce-mean	LR decay start	9	Skip connections	True
RNN size	300	Vocab size src/tgt	80/150	Clip normalization	3	Layer normalization	True
Epochs	15	Optimizer	adam				

2.4 Evaluation Procedure

Produced DRSs are compared with the gold standard representations by using COUNTER (Van Noord, Abzianidze, Haagsma, and Bos, 2018). This is a tool that calculates micro precision, recall and F-score over matching clauses, similar to the SMATCH (Cai and Knight, 2013) evaluation tool for AMR parsing. All clauses have the same weight in matching, except for REF clauses, which are ignored.

An example of the matching procedure is shown in Figure 1. The produced DRSs go through a strict syntactic and semantic validation process, as described in Van Noord, Abzianidze, Toral, and Bos (2018). If a produced DRS is invalid, it is replaced by a dummy DRS, which gets an F-score of 0.0.

We check whether two systems differ significantly by performing approximate randomization (Noreen, 1989), with $\alpha = 0.05$, $R = 1000$ and $F(model_1) > F(model_2)$ as test statistic for each DRS pair.

3 Results and Discussion

We perform all our experiments twice: (i) only using gold data for training and (ii) with both gold (fully manually annotated) and silver (partially manually annotated) data.

The results of adding external sources of linguistic information are shown in Table 4. We clearly see that using an additional encoder for the linguistic information is superior to merging all the information in a single encoder. For two encoders and only using gold data, the scores increase by at least 0.7 for each source of information individually. Lemmatization shows the highest improvement, most likely because the DRS concepts that need to be produced are often lemmatized versions of the source words. When we stack the linguistic features, we observe an improvement for each addition, resulting in a final 2.7 point F-score increase over the baseline.

If we also employ silver data, we again observe that the multi-encoder setup is preferable over a single encoder, for both isolating and stacking the linguistic features. On isolation, the results are similar to only using gold data, with the exception of the semantic tags, which even hurt the performance now. Interestingly, when stacking the linguistic features, there is no improvement over only using the lemma of the source words.

We now compare our best models to previous parsers[4] (Bos, 2015; Van Noord, Abzianidze, Toral, and Bos, 2018) and two baseline systems, SPAR and SIM-SPAR. As previously indicated, Van Noord, Abzianidze, Toral, and Bos (2018) used a similar sequence-to-sequence model as our current approach, but implemented in OpenNMT and without the linguistic features. Boxer (Bos, 2008, 2015) is a DRS parser that uses a statistical CCG parser for syntactic analysis and a compositional semantics based on λ-calculus, followed by pronoun and presupposition resolution. SPAR is a baseline system that outputs the same DRS for each test instance[5], while SIM-SPAR outputs the DRS of the most similar sentence in the training set, based on a simple word embedding metric.[6] The results are shown in Table 5. Our model clearly outperforms the previous systems, even when only using gold standard data. When compared to Van Noord, Abzianidze, Toral, and Bos (2018), retrained with the same data used in our systems,

---

[4]Since Liu et al. (2018) used data from the Groningen Meaning Bank instead of the PMB, we cannot make a comparison.

[5]For PMB release 2.2.0 this is the DRS for *Tom voted for himself.*

[6]See Section 5.1 of Van Noord, Abzianidze, Haagsma, and Bos (2018) for an explanation of the high baseline scores.

Table 4: Table (a) and (b) show the results of adding **a single type** of linguistic information. Table (c) and (d) show the results for **stacking multiple types** of linguistic information. Reported scores are F-scores on the development set, averaged over 5 runs of the system, with confidence scores.

(a)	Gold only: single type	
Model	**1 enc**	**2 enc**
Baseline	78.6 ± 0.6	NA
POS-tags	**79.5 ± 0.8**	79.3 ± 0.6
Semantic tags	79.0 ± 0.9	79.3 ± 0.4
Lemma	78.6 ± 0.4	**79.9 ± 0.4**
Dependency parse	78.9 ± 0.7	79.3 ± 0.8
CCG supertags	78.6 ± 1.1	79.4 ± 0.9

(b)	Gold + silver: single type	
Model	**1 enc**	**2 enc**
Baseline	84.5 ± 0.3	NA
POS tags	**84.8 ± 0.3**	84.9 ± 0.4
Semantic tags	83.5 ± 0.6	84.0 ± 0.4
Lemma	84.0 ± 0.2	**85.6 ± 0.4**
Dependency parse	83.9 ± 0.4	84.6 ± 0.3
CCG supertags	83.8 ± 0.3	84.8 ± 0.5

(c)	Gold only: stacking	
Model	**1 enc**	**2 enc**
Baseline	78.6 ± 0.6	NA
+ Lemma	78.6 ± 0.4	79.9 ± 0.4
+ Semantic tags	**79.4 ± 0.6**	80.5 ± 0.6
+ POS tags	79.4 ± 0.3	80.8 ± 0.3
+ CCG supertags	79.4 ± 0.6	81.0 ± 0.6
+ Dependency parse	78.8 ± 0.7	**81.3 ± 0.9**

(d)	Gold + silver: stacking	
Model	**1 enc**	**2 enc**
Baseline	**84.5 ± 0.3**	NA
+ Lemma	84.0 ± 0.2	**85.6 ± 0.4**
+ POS-tags	84.3 ± 0.4	85.5 ± 0.3
+ CCG supertags	84.5 ± 0.2	85.6 ± 0.6
+ Dependency parse	84.5 ± 0.2	85.4 ± 0.4
+ Semantic tags	83.7 ± 0.4	85.1 ± 0.2

the largest improvement (3.6 and 3.5 for dev and test) comes from switching framework and changing certain parameters such as the optimizer and learning rate. However, the linguistic features are clearly still beneficial when using only gold data (increase of 2.7 and 1.9 for dev and test), and also still help when employing additional silver data (1.1 and 0.3 increase for dev and test, both significant).

Table 5: Results on the test set compared to a number of baseline parsers and the Seq2seq OpenNMT model of Van Noord, Abzianidze, Toral, and Bos (2018). Our scores are averages of 5 runs, with confidence scores.

	Dev			Test		
	Prec	**Rec**	**F-score**	**Prec**	**Rec**	**F-score**
SPAR	42.3	37.9	40.0	44.4	37.8	40.8
SIM-SPAR	52.4	54.2	53.3	57.0	58.4	57.7
Boxer (Bos, 2015)	72.5	72.0	72.2	72.1	72.3	72.2
Van Noord, Abzianidze, Toral, and Bos (2018)	83.5	78.5	80.9	85.0	81.4	83.2
This paper: gold only	81.9	75.6	78.6 ± 0.6	85.1	78.1	81.5 ± 0.2
This paper: gold only + all ling	84.3	78.5	81.3 ± 0.9	86.6	80.4	83.4 ± 0.4
This paper: gold + silver	85.9	83.2	84.5 ± 0.3	87.4	86.0	86.7 ± 0.2
This paper: gold + silver + lemma	86.5	84.8	85.6 ± 0.4	87.6	86.3	87.0 ± 0.4

4   Conclusions

In this paper we have shown that a range of linguistic features can improve performance of sequence-to-sequence models for the task of parsing Discourse Representation Structures. We have shown empirically that the best method of adding these features is by using a multi-encoder setup, as opposed to merging the sources of linguistic information in a single encoder. We believe that this method can also be beneficial for other semantic parsing tasks in which sequence-to-sequence models do well.

References

Abzianidze, L., J. Bjerva, K. Evang, H. Haagsma, R. van Noord, P. Ludmann, D.-D. Nguyen, and J. Bos (2017, April). The Parallel Meaning Bank: Towards a multilingual corpus of translations annotated with compositional meaning representations. In *Proceedings of the 15th Conference of the European Chapter of the Association for Computational Linguistics: Volume 2, Short Papers*, Valencia, Spain, pp. 242–247. Association for Computational Linguistics.

Abzianidze, L. and J. Bos (2017, September). Towards universal semantic tagging. In *Proceedings of the 12th International Conference on Computational Semantics (IWCS 2017) – Short Papers*, Montpellier, France, pp. 307–313. Association for Computational Linguistics.

Aharoni, R. and Y. Goldberg (2017). Towards string-to-tree neural machine translation. In *Proceedings of the 55th Annual Meeting of the Association for Computational Linguistics (Volume 2: Short Papers)*, pp. 132–140. Association for Computational Linguistics.

Bahdanau, D., K. Cho, and Y. Bengio (2014). Neural machine translation by jointly learning to align and translate. *CoRR abs/1409.0473*.

Bjerva, J., B. Plank, and J. Bos (2016). Semantic tagging with deep residual networks. In *Proceedings of COLING 2016, the 26th International Conference on Computational Linguistics: Technical Papers*, Osaka, Japan, pp. 3531–3541.

Bos, J. (2008). Wide-coverage semantic analysis with Boxer. In *Semantics in Text Processing. STEP 2008 Conference Proceedings*, Volume 1 of *Research in Computational Semantics*, pp. 277–286. Venice, Italy: College Publications.

Bos, J. (2015). Open-domain semantic parsing with Boxer. In B. Megyesi (Ed.), *Proceedings of the 20th Nordic Conference of Computational Linguistics (NODALIDA 2015)*, Vilnius, Lithuania, pp. 301–304.

Brants, T. (2000). Tnt: A statistical part-of-speech tagger. In *Proceedings of the Sixth Conference on Applied Natural Language Processing*, ANLC '00, Stroudsburg, PA, USA, pp. 224–231. Association for Computational Linguistics.

Cai, S. and K. Knight (2013, August). Smatch: An evaluation metric for semantic feature structures. In *Proceedings of the 51st Annual Meeting of the Association for Computational Linguistics (Volume 2: Short Papers)*, Sofia, Bulgaria, pp. 748–752. Association for Computational Linguistics.

Currey, A. and K. Heafield (2018). Multi-source syntactic neural machine translation. In *Proceedings of the 2018 Conference on Empirical Methods in Natural Language Processing*, pp. 2961–2966. Association for Computational Linguistics.

de Bruijn, N. G. (1972). Lambda calculus notation with nameless dummies, a tool for automatic formula manipulation, with application to the church-rosser theorem. In *Indagationes Mathematicae (Proceedings)*, Volume 75, pp. 381–392. Elsevier.

Dong, L. and M. Lapata (2018). Coarse-to-fine decoding for neural semantic parsing. In *Proceedings of the 56th Annual Meeting of the Association for Computational Linguistics (Volume 1: Long Papers)*, pp. 731–742. Association for Computational Linguistics.

Duong, L., H. Afshar, D. Estival, G. Pink, P. Cohen, and M. Johnson (2017). Multilingual semantic parsing and code-switching. In *Proceedings of the 21st Conference on Computational Natural Language Learning (CoNLL 2017)*, pp. 379–389.

Firat, O., K. Cho, and Y. Bengio (2016). Multi-way, multilingual neural machine translation with a shared attention mechanism. In *Proceedings of NAACL-HLT*, pp. 866–875.

Jia, R. and P. Liang (2016). Data recombination for neural semantic parsing. In *Proceedings of the 54th Annual Meeting of the Association for Computational Linguistics (Volume 1: Long Papers)*, Volume 1, Berlin, Germany, pp. 12–22.

Junczys-Dowmunt, M., R. Grundkiewicz, T. Dwojak, H. Hoang, K. Heafield, T. Neckermann, F. Seide, U. Germann, A. Fikri Aji, N. Bogoychev, A. F. T. Martins, and A. Birch (2018, July). Marian: Fast neural machine translation in C++. In *Proceedings of ACL 2018, System Demonstrations*, Melbourne, Australia, pp. 116–121. Association for Computational Linguistics.

Kamp, H. and U. Reyle (1993). *From Discourse to Logic; An Introduction to Modeltheoretic Semantics of Natural Language, Formal Logic and DRT*. Dordrecht: Kluwer.

Klein, G., Y. Kim, Y. Deng, J. Senellart, and A. Rush (2017). OpenNMT: Open-source toolkit for neural machine translation. In *Proceedings of ACL 2017, System Demonstrations*, Vancouver, Canada, pp. 67–72. Association for Computational Linguistics.

Konstas, I., S. Iyer, M. Yatskar, Y. Choi, and L. Zettlemoyer (2017, July). Neural AMR: Sequence-to-sequence models for parsing and generation. In *Proceedings of the 55th Annual Meeting of the Association for Computational Linguistics (Volume 1: Long Papers)*, Vancouver, Canada, pp. 146–157. Association for Computational Linguistics.

Lewis, M. and M. Steedman (2014). A* CCG parsing with a supertag-factored model. In *Proceedings of the 2014 Conference on Empirical Methods in Natural Language Processing (EMNLP)*, Doha, Qatar, pp. 990–1000.

Libovický, J. and J. Helcl (2017). Attention strategies for multi-source sequence-to-sequence learning. In *Proceedings of the 55th Annual Meeting of the Association for Computational Linguistics (Volume 2: Short Papers)*, pp. 196–202. Association for Computational Linguistics.

Ling, W., P. Blunsom, E. Grefenstette, K. M. Hermann, T. Kočiský, F. Wang, and A. Senior (2016). Latent predictor networks for code generation. In *Proceedings of the 54th Annual Meeting of the Association for Computational Linguistics (Volume 1: Long Papers)*, Volume 1, Berlin, Germany, pp. 599–609.

Liu, J., S. B. Cohen, and M. Lapata (2018). Discourse representation structure parsing. In *Proceedings of the 56th Annual Meeting of the Association for Computational Linguistics (Volume 1: Long Papers)*, Volume 1, Melbourne, Australia, pp. 429–439.

Manning, C., M. Surdeanu, J. Bauer, J. Finkel, S. Bethard, and D. McClosky (2014). The stanford corenlp natural language processing toolkit. In *Proceedings of 52nd annual meeting of the association for computational linguistics: system demonstrations*, pp. 55–60.

Noreen, E. W. (1989). *Computer-intensive Methods for Testing Hypotheses*. Wiley New York.

Sennrich, R. and B. Haddow (2016). Linguistic input features improve neural machine translation. In *Proceedings of the First Conference on Machine Translation: Volume 1, Research Papers*, Volume 1, pp. 83–91.

Susanto, R. H. and W. Lu (2017). Neural architectures for multilingual semantic parsing. In *Proceedings of the 55th Annual Meeting of the Association for Computational Linguistics (Volume 2: Short Papers)*, Volume 2, pp. 38–44.

Van Noord, R., L. Abzianidze, H. Haagsma, and J. Bos (2018). Evaluating scoped meaning representations. In *Proceedings of the Eleventh International Conference on Language Resources and Evaluation (LREC 2018)*, Paris, France, pp. 1685–1693. European Language Resources Association (ELRA).

Van Noord, R., L. Abzianidze, A. Toral, and J. Bos (2018). Exploring neural methods for parsing discourse representation structures. *Transactions of the Association for Computational Linguistics 6*, 619–633.

Van Noord, R. and J. Bos (2017a). Dealing with co-reference in neural semantic parsing. In *Proceedings of the 2nd Workshop on Semantic Deep Learning (SemDeep-2)*, Montpellier, France, pp. 41–49.

Van Noord, R. and J. Bos (2017b). Neural semantic parsing by character-based translation: Experiments with abstract meaning representations. *Computational Linguistics in the Netherlands Journal 7*, 93–108.

Zoph, B. and K. Knight (2016). Multi-source neural translation. In *Proceedings of NAACL-HLT*, pp. 30–34.

Making sense of conflicting (defeasible) rules in the controlled natural language ACE: design of a system with support for existential quantification using skolemization[*]

Martin Diller
TU Wien, Austria
mdiller@kr.tuwien.ac.at

Adam Wyner
Swansea University, Wales
a.z.wyner@swansea.ac.uk

Hannes Strass
Leipzig University, Germany
strass@informatik.uni-leipzig.de

Abstract

We present the design of a system for making sense of conflicting rules expressed in a fragment of the prominent controlled natural language ACE, yet extended with means of expressing defeasible rules in the form of normality assumptions. The approach we describe is ultimately based on answer-set-programming (ASP); simulating existential quantification by using skolemization in a manner resembling a translation for ASP recently formalized in the context of $\exists$-ASP. We discuss the advantages of this approach to building on the existing ACE interface to rule-systems, ACERules.

1 Introduction

Attempto Controlled English (ACE) (Fuchs et al., 2008) is a prominent controlled natural language (CNL) for knowledge representation (KR). Apart of its appropriateness for basic KR, ACE's attraction comes, first of all, from its ties with formal logic: ACE texts have an unambiguous translation to first order logic (FOL). Secondly, there are several open-source tools for ACE; the main one being the parser APE, which translates ACE texts to FOL via discourse representation structures (DRSs) (Blackburn and Bos, 2005) and also verbalises DRSs.

Our interest is in the adaptation of ACE for handling conflicting information expressed in the form of strict and defeasible rules. In (Diller et al., 2017) we outlined a methodology for this task, which we more recently dubbed the EMIL ("Extracting Meaning out of Inconsistent Language") pipeline. The pipeline starts out with rules expressed in ACE (ACE rules), yet extended with means of expressing defeasible rules; currently, in the form of normality assumptions ("it is usual that"). We transform ACE rules to defeasible theories that can be evaluated via the direct stable semantics as defined in (Strass and Wyner, 2017). We verbalise possible manners of making sense of the rules (the "stable sets"), again, by making use of ACE.

In (Diller et al., 2017) we report on an adaptation of the main existing open-source interface to rule systems for ACE, ACERules (Kuhn, 2007), for our purposes[1]. At the back-end we used the ASP encodings for the direct stable semantics reported on in (Strass and Wyner, 2017). Here we motivate and

---

[*]This work has been funded by the Austrian Science Fund (FWF) projects I2854 and W1255-N23; also by the German Research Foundation (DFG) project 389792660 - TRR 248.

[1]This line of study has been continued via the PENG^{ASP} system (Guy and Schwitter, 2017), which as far as we are able to tell, inherits many of the features (while also improving on several others; e.g. in one of the more recent iterations, using a bi-directional grammar for specifying and verbalising ASP-programs (Schwitter, 2018)) of ACERules (in particular, that it does not offer explicit support of existential quantification) yet is not open-source nor publicly available for experimentation.

sketch the design of an alternative implementation of the EMIL pipeline. We, first of all, target short-comings we found in the transformations that `ACERules` carries out for making `APE` parses ammenable to handling by rule systems. We refer to these in Section 2 and our alternative approach in Section 3. The main difference between the approach we present here and that based on `ACERules` is that `ACERules` attempts to remove existential variables whenever possible and filters-out ACE texts composed of rules it cannot handle. We here, on the other hand, simulate rules with existential quantification using skolem-ization in a manner resembling the procedure formalised in the context of $\exists$-ASP (Garreau et al., 2015) (see Section 3.1). A second difference is that we use dynamic encodings of the direct-stable-semantics to ASP, optimised for defeasible theories with function symbols (Section 3.2). For an extended presentation we refer to Chapter 4 of (Diller, 2019).

2 `ACERules` and its transformations

`AceRules` builds on `APE` to provide an ACE interface to formal rule systems. The system works by first checking the parses from `APE` , filtering those that amount to what we, following Garreau et al.[2], will call $\exists$-rules[3]. In their most general form, these have the form

$$b_1, \ldots, b_m, \triangle(n_1^1, \ldots, n_{u_1}^1), \ldots, \triangle(n_1^s, \ldots, n_{u_s}^s) \triangleright H$$

where $\triangleright$ is $\rightarrow$ ("strict implication") and H is of the form $h_1, \ldots, h_t$ or $\neg(h_1, \ldots, h_t)$. Also, $h_1, \ldots, h_t$, $b_1, \ldots, b_m, n_1^1, \ldots, n_{u_1}^1, \ldots, n_1^s, \ldots, n_{u_s}^s$ are atoms with constants and variables as usual in logic pro-grams (Brewka et al., 2011), $m, s \geq 0$, and $t, u_1, \ldots, u_s \geq 1$. Moreover, $\triangle \in \{\texttt{not}, \texttt{not}\neg, \neg\}$ with $\neg$ standing for strong negation and $\texttt{not}$ standing for negation-as-failure. Variables in $n_1^1, \ldots, n_{u_1}^1$ to $n_1^s, \ldots, n_{u_s}^s$ but not in $b_1, \ldots, b_m$ are interpreted as existentially quantified. The same for variables in the head H but not in $b_1, \ldots, b_m$. In the implementation from (Diller et al., 2017), dACERules, we modi-fied `APE` to recognise "it is usual that" as a form of subordination on the par with modal constructs. We thus also allow $\triangleright$ to be $\Rightarrow$ ("defeasible implication"). On the other hand, we disallow negation-as-failure.

    `ACERules` (and thus dACERules) filters DRSs corresponding to $\exists$-rules rather than normal rules (i.e. $u_i = 1$ for $0 \leq i \leq s$, $t = 1$, and there are no existentially quantified variables) because most meaningful examples of ACE rules require the additional resources provided by $\exists$-rules. The reason is not only that $\exists$-rules are natural, but also due to the flat form of logical atoms used by `APE` (Fuchs et al., 2013). I.e. a sentence such as "Mary gladly gives John a present" is represented as

$$\exists A, B \big(object(A, present, countable, na, eq, 1) \wedge modifier\_adv(B, gladly, pos) \wedge$$
$$predicate(B, give, named(Mary), A, named(John)))$$

where e.g. nouns, verbs, and adverbs are "wrapped" into the special atoms "object", "predicate", "mod-ifier_adv". These have additional arguments encoding semantic information. Critical for our purposes is that only noun phrases and verb phrases introduce referents (quantified variables); the remaining pred-icates make use of the referents introduced by noun and verb phrases. In particular, verb phrases have a Neo-Davidsonian event-theoretic semantics (Parsons, 1990), allowing to attach modifiers stemming from adverbs and prepositional phrases to the referents introduced by verb phrases (in the example "B").

    In order to make ACE texts parsed as $\exists$-rules ammenable to processing by rule systems , `ACERules` implements a series of transformations of the $\exists$-rules; the main ones being predicate condensation and grouping (only the latter is discussed in (Kuhn, 2007)). Predicate condensation merges atoms for verb phrases and their modifiers, grouping them in a single atom $pred\_mod$; the referent for the verb is removed. E.g. for the example above the result of predicate condensation is:

$$pred\_mod(give, named(Mary), A, named(John), [modifier\_adv(gladly, pos)])$$

The problem with this transformation is that it modifies the semantics of the parse given by APE: the "di-amond inference pattern" holding between a verb phrase plus modifiers and its components (see Parsons (1990)) is broken. So e.g. the output given by `ACERules` for the text (adapted from Parsons (1990))

---

[2]Although they do not consider strong negation.
[3]`ACERules` also transforms rules with double implication to equivalent $\exists$-rules.

```
Brutus unhesitatingly stabs Caeser in the back with a knife.
If Brutus stabs Caeser then Brutus is a traitor.
```

does not include the assertion that Brutus is a traitor[4] since `ACERules` is unable to relate "Brutus stabs Caeser" with "Brutus unhesitatingly stabs Caeser in the back with a knife".

After postprocessing condensed atoms for the copula "be" and the preposition "of" (see (Diller, 2019)), the main transformation carried out by `ACERules` is "grouping", which amounts to aggregating atoms appearing in the heads of ∃-rules or negated (via ¬, not ¬, or not) in the bodies of rules when possible. Atoms appearing in other parts of the parse of `APE`, yet which match some of the grouped atoms, are likewise grouped together ("matching phase"). Existentially quantified variables in the grouped atoms are removed subject to the to the restriction that the variable is not used elsewhere in the parse, outside of the group of atoms. An example of rules that can be treated by grouping are (from (Kuhn, 2007)):

```
John owns a car.
Bill does not own a car.
If someone does not own a car then he/she owns a house.
```

Here atoms for "owns a car" and "owns a house" are merged in a single atom (denoting "owns-a-car" and "owns-a-house") and the variables referring to the car and house respectively are removed. If after "John owns a car" one adds the sentence "Mary sees the car" grouping fails as reference to a car independent of someone owning it is needed. See (Kuhn, 2007) and (Diller, 2019) for further details.

Apart from groups of atoms being treated as lists rather than sets in `ACERules`[5], we found the checks for grouping to succeed to be too liberal. As an example, the matching phase only considers groups of atoms that match exactly, while often also sub-groups need to be considered. E.g., consider:

```
John owns a car.
Every car is an automobile.
John does not own an automobile.
```

`ACERules` groups atoms for "John owns an automobile" and then is unable to relate "owning a car" with "owning an automobile" concluding that John owns a car but not an automobile.

The matching phase in `ACERules` also does not consider groups matching in terms of the atoms but differing in generality. An example of a text where this is necessary is:

```
Bill does not own a vehicle.
If Bill does not own a vehicle then he does not own a car.
If someone does not own a car then he/she owns a motorcycle.
If someone owns a motorcycle then he/she owns a vehicle.
```

`ACERules` is unable to relate the group of atoms for "Bill owns a vehicle" and the more general (because of the use of an indefinite pronoun) "he/she owns a vehicle" concluding that it is both true and false that John owns a vehicle.

More minor issues we found in our study of `ACERules` are that transformations introduced for indefinite pronouns blur the distinction between inanimate objects and persons[6] and post-processing of condensed atoms for the copula "be" favours an intersective reading of adjectives[7].

3   A system with support for existential quantification using skolemization

We have shown in Section 2 that several of the transformations implemented in `ACERules`, particularly predicate-condensation and grouping, introduce significant deviations from the semantics of ACE rules induced by `APE`. Moreover, even in the current rather liberal implementation of grouping, the texts `ACERules` can handle are limited; especially, often existential quantification is unavoidable.

---

[4]While, for instance, the first order reasoner for ACE, RACE (Fuchs, 2010), finds a proof of "Brutus is a traitor" from the same text. Another issue with predicate condensation, which is more likely a bug than an intended feature of `ACERules`, is that modifiers in the *pred_mod* predicates are aggregated into ordered lists, while their semantics (at least as given by the parse by `APE`) would require them to be aggregated into sets.

[5]This bug is documented in the source-code of `ACERules`.

[6]Thus, e.g., from "there is a table" and "everybody likes Mary" `ACERules` concludes that "the table [X1] likes Mary".

[7]For instance (example adapted from `https://www3.nd.edu/~jspeaks/courses/2012-13/43916/handouts/13-modifiers.pdf`; accessed on 28.11.2018) `ACERules` reads the subsective adjective "tall" intersectively in the discourse composed of the sentences "Bob is a tall midget", "Bob is a basketball-player", and "if Bob is a tall basketball-player then he plays for the NBA"; concluding that Bob plays for the NBA.

3.1 From strict and defeasible ∃-rules to normal rules

The most obvious manner of supporting existential quantification in rules is by using skolemization in normal-rules to simulate the latter; for ASP this approach has recently been formalised in the context of ∃-ASP (Garreau et al., 2015). Although the original definitions for defeasible theories from (Strass and Wyner, 2017) do not allow function symbols these can be incorporated without further ado; in fact, the ASP-encodings reported on in (Strass and Wyner, 2017) support them. Having function symbols, we can thus compile strict and defeasible ∃-rules (without `not`) to normal defeasible theories in a manner similar to that proposed in (Garreau et al., 2015) for transforming ∃-rules into normal ASP programs. Differences are due to the fact that we have strong negation rather than negation-as-failure (in (Garreau et al., 2015) strong negation is not considered) and defeasible implication in addition to strict implication.

The translation of strict ∃-rules with positive elements in the body and head is exactly as in (Garreau et al., 2015); defeasible rules introduce the issue of deciding the scope of "⇒". Consider, for instance:

```
It is usual that a ferry that starts in Vienna services Bratislava.
```

In our translation the rule gets replaced by the unary assumption with an auxilliary atom:

$$\Rightarrow x\_auxPH1()$$

accompanied by auxilliary rules introducing skolem constants (e.g. x_sk1) for the objects and verbs[8]:

$$x\_auxPH1() \rhd_1 object(x\_sk1(), ferry)$$
$$x\_auxPH1() \rhd_2 predicate(x\_sk2(), start, x\_sk1())$$
$$x\_auxPH1() \rhd_3 modifier\_pp(x\_sk2(), in, vienna)$$
$$x\_auxPH1() \rhd_4 predicate(x\_sk3(), service, x\_sk1(), bratislava)$$

Having $\rhd_i$ being $\rightarrow$ for each i ($1 \leq i \leq 4$) amounts to interpreting the scope of $\Rightarrow$ to be over the entire phrase "a ferry that starts in Vienna services Bratislava". We currently implement this option, but a more satisfactory reading may be that there usually is a ferry that either starts in Vienna or services Bratislava (and, typically, both). This option can be encoded using further auxilliary atoms (see (Diller, 2019)).

Turning to ∃-rules with negated atoms in the head, consider the sentence "if someone owns a car then he/she does not own a house". In our translation we once more replace the head of the ∃-rule obtained from the APE parse with an auxilliary atom:

$$object(A, somebody), object(B, car), predicate(C, own, A, B) \rightarrow x\_auxNH1(A, B, C)$$

and add rules encoding the meaning of the auxilliary atom:

$$object(D, house), x\_auxNH1(A, B, C), pName(E) \rightarrow \neg predicate(E, own, A, D)$$
$$predicate(E, own, A, D), x\_auxNH1(A, B, C) \rightarrow \neg object(D, house)$$

Here the use of the special atom $pName$ (which collects all variables standing for verbs) is optional, but used for the first rule to be safe (i.e. all variables occurring in the head occur in the body). If there are more than two atoms appearing negated in the head of a rule we need to apply the illustrated translation recursively. Note also that the treatment of defeasible rules with negative heads is exactly analogous to that of strict rules. The reason is that $\Rightarrow$ inherits the scope from $\neg$ in this case.

A conceptually more intricate case is when negation occurs in atypical manner in the bodies of rules, e.g. for the sentence "if someone does not own a car then he/she owns a house". Here there are several options. The most straightforward, following more or less (Garreau et al., 2015), is to put the burden of proof on the existential assertion; i.e. by default no one owns a car. This option, which is the one we currently implement, can be encoded as follows (omitting the auxilliary rules for x_auxPH1) :

$$object(A, somebody), \neg x\_auxPB1(A) \rightarrow x\_auxPH1(A)$$
$$object(B, car), predicate(C, own, A, B) \rightarrow x\_auxPB1(A)$$
$$object(A, somebody) \Rightarrow \neg x\_auxPB1(A)$$

One can also put the burden of proof on the negation of the existential assertion (see (Diller, 2019)), but arguably more in line with the framework of (Strass and Wyner, 2017) is to reason by cases; i.e.

---

[8]For readability we use a simpler representation of the atoms to that of APE.

consider for everyone both the possibility that the he/she owns a car and that he/she does not. One simple encoding of this option is as follows:

$$object(A, somebody), \neg x\_auxPB1(A) \to x\_auxPH1(A)$$
$$object(A, somebody) \Rightarrow \neg x\_auxPB1(A)$$
$$object(A, somebody) \Rightarrow x\_auxPB1(A)$$
$$x\_auxPB1(A) \to object(x\_sk1(A), house)$$
$$x\_auxPB1(A) \to predicate(x\_sk2(A), own, A, x\_sk1(A))$$
$$\neg x\_auxPB1(A), predicate(C, own, A, B) \to \neg object(B, house)$$
$$\neg x\_auxPB1(A), object(B, house), pName(C) \to \neg predicate(C, own, A, B)$$

3.2 Dynamic ASP encoding for defeasible theories with variables

The ASP encoding for evaluating (normal) defeasible theories[9] via the direct stable semantics we used in the implementation of the EMIL pipeline reported on in (Diller et al., 2017) is static: only the part specifying the defeasible theory changes with the input. The module for the semantic evaluation uses ASP-disjunction and remains fixed. The encoding is thus complexity-sensitive for propositional defeasible theories (the complexity of the latter and the data complexity of disjunctive ASP is Σ_2^P-complete).

For theories with variables the encoding nevertheless has the disadvantage that defeasible theories need to be specified essentially as facts and hence the grounding (transformation of defeasible theories with variables to theories without variables; see (Strass and Wyner, 2017)) needs to be generated explicitly (in most cases) while this is usually not the case for ASP programs with variables (Kaufmann et al., 2016). This is even more a problem when using function symbols, which introduce the possibility of infinite groundings. For instance, the defeasible theory $\{\to o(a), o(X) \to p(f(X)), p(X) \to q(f(X))\}$ has the unique stable set $\{a, p(f(a)), q(f(a))\}$, which as an ASP program is computed in under one second[10] by e.g. the ASP-solver `clingo` (5.3.0) (Gebser et al., 2018). When evaluating the theory in the context of the encodings from (Strass and Wyner, 2017) via `clingo` there are memory errors (”std::bad_alloc”) after 48.566 seconds.

For the mentioned reason, we developed alternative dynamic (both the data and program change with the input), yet structure-preserving ASP encodings for evaluating defeasible theories with variables via the direct-stable-semantics for our new implementation of the EMIL pipeline. Such encodings allow us to piggyback on the grounding developments for any ASP grounder (+ solver) we wish to experiment with. Moreover, the encodings are to non-disjunctive ASP. We refer to (Diller, 2019) for details.

4 Discussion and future work

We have outlined an alternative design for a system for making sense of conflicting rules in the CNL ACE. The main component is a translation from (defeasible) ∃-rules to normal rules which can be seen as a form of meaning-preserving grouping, subsuming a form of predicate-condensation. In particular, the latter does not break the relation between verbs and their modifiers (via the use of auxilliary rules and skolemization) (see the examples in Section 3.1). The second component is the dynamic ASP encoding optimised for evaluating defeasible theories with variables.

We have an implementation working[11]. Immediate future work is to add support for generating arguments from defeasible theories and experimenting with ASP grounders and solvers. More future plans are incorporation of means of restricting existential variables whenever possible (in the spirit of `ACERules`) and/or restrictions to ensure finite groundability. Further long term goals are investigation of alternative means of supporting existential quantification, support of different forms of adding defeasibility to ACE, and enhancing the natural language understanding capabilities of our system.

---

[9] `https://github.com/hstrass/defeasible-rules`

[10] On a 4 GB openSUSE (42.3) machine with 4 Intel Core processors (3.30 GHz).

[11] We have been able to successfully run (in under one minute) most test-cases (with some modifications in case of there being negation-as-failure as well as priorities over rules) available for `AceRules` (around 40 of them). The implementation is available at `https://www.dbai.tuwien.ac.at/proj/grappa/emil/`. An upcoming version will include treatment of the copula “be” and the preposition “of”; in the first case modifying and in the second case incorporating the treatment of `ACERules` (see (Diller, 2019)).

References

Blackburn, P. and J. Bos (2005). *Representation and Inference for Natural Language: A First Course in Computational Semantics*. CSLI Publications.

Brewka, G., T. Eiter, and M. Truszczynski (2011). Answer set programming at a glance. *Commun. ACM 54*(12), 92–103.

Diller, M. (2019). *Realising argumentation using answer set programming and quantified boolean formulas*. Ph. D. thesis, Vienna University of Technology. Submitted.

Diller, M., A. Wyner, and H. Strass (2017, September). Defeasible AceRules: A prototype. In C. Gardent and C. Retoré (Eds.), *Proceedings of the 12th International Conference on Computational Semantics (IWCS 2017)*.

Fuchs, N. E. (2010). First-Order Reasoning for Attempto Controlled English. In M. Rosner and N. E. Fuchs (Eds.), *Proceedings of the 2nd International Workshop on Controlled Natural Language (CNL 2010)*, Volume 7175 of *Lecture Notes in Computer Science*, pp. 73–94. Springer.

Fuchs, N. E., K. Kaljurand, and T. Kuhn (2008). Attempto Controlled English for knowledge representation. In *Tutorial lectures of the 4th International Summer School on the Reasoning Web (Reasoning Web 2008)*, pp. 104–124.

Fuchs, N. E., K. Kaljurand, and T. Kuhn (2013). Discourse Representation Structures for ACE 6.7. Technical report. Available at `http://attempto.ifi.uzh.ch/site/pubs/papers/drs_report_67.pdf`.

Garreau, F., L. Garcia, C. Lefèvre, and I. Stéphan (2015). $\exists$-ASP. In *Proceedings of the Joint Ontology Workshops 2015 Episode 1: The Argentine Winter of Ontology co-located with the 24th International Joint Conference on Artificial Intelligence (IJCAI 2015)*, Volume 1517 of *CEUR Workshop Proceedings*. CEUR-WS.org.

Gebser, M., R. Kaminski, B. Kaufmann, P. Lühne, P. Obermeier, M. Ostrowski, J. Romero, T. Schaub, S. Schellhorn, and P. Wanko (2018). The Potsdam Answer Set Solving Collection 5.0. *KI 32*(2-3), 181–182.

Guy, S. and R. Schwitter (2017). The PENG ASP system: architecture, language and authoring tool. *Language Resources and Evaluation 51*(1), 67–92.

Kaufmann, B., N. Leone, S. Perri, and T. Schaub (2016). Grounding and solving in answer set programming. *AI Magazine 37*(3), 25–32.

Kuhn, T. (2007). AceRules: Executing Rules in Controlled Natural Language. In *Proceedings of the 1rst International Conference on Web Reasoning and Rule Systems (RR 2007)*, Volume 4524 of *Lecture Notes in Computer Science*, pp. 299–308. Springer.

Parsons, T. (1990). *Events in the Semantics of English: A Study of Subatomic Semantics* (1s ed.). Cambridge, MA, USA: MIT Press.

Schwitter, R. (2018). Specifying and Verbalising Answer Set Programs in Controlled Natural Language. *TPLP 18*(3-4), 691–705.

Strass, H. and A. Wyner (2017, February). On Automated Defeasible Reasoning with Controlled Natural Language and Argumentation. In R. Barták, T. L. McCluskey, and E. Pontelli (Eds.), *Proceedings of the 2nd International Workshop on Knowledge-based Techniques for Problem Solving and Reasoning (KnowProS 2017)*.

Distributional Interaction of Concreteness and Abstractness in Verb–Noun Subcategorisation

Diego Frassinelli, Sabine Schulte im Walde
Institut für Maschinelle Sprachverarbeitung
Universität Stuttgart
[frassinelli|schulte]@ims.uni-stuttgart.de

Abstract

In recent years, both cognitive and computational research has provided empirical analyses of contextual co-occurrence of concrete and abstract words, partially resulting in inconsistent pictures. In this work we provide a more fine-grained description of the distributional nature in the corpus-based interaction of verbs and nouns within subcategorisation, by investigating the concreteness of verbs and nouns that are in a specific syntactic relationship with each other, i.e., subject, direct object, and prepositional object. Overall, our experiments show consistent patterns in the distributional representation of subcategorising and subcategorised concrete and abstract words. At the same time, the studies reveal empirical evidence why contextual abstractness represents a valuable indicator for automatic non-literal language identification.

1 Introduction

The need of providing a clear description of the usage of concrete and abstract words in communication is becoming salient both in cognitive science and in computational linguistics. In the cognitive science community, much has been said about concrete concepts, but there is still an open debate about the nature of abstract concepts (Barsalou and Wiemer-Hastings, 2005; McRae and Jones, 2013; Hill et al., 2014; Vigliocco et al., 2014). Computational linguists have recognised the importance of investigating the concreteness of contexts in empirical models, for example for the automatic identification of non-literal language usage (Turney et al., 2011; Köper and Schulte im Walde, 2016; Aedmaa et al., 2018).

Recently, multiple studies have focussed on providing a fine-grained analysis of the nature of concrete vs. abstract words from a corpus-based perspective (Bhaskar et al., 2017; Frassinelli et al., 2017; Naumann et al., 2018). In these studies, the authors have shown a general but consistent pattern: concrete words have a preference to co-occur with other concrete words, while abstract words co-occur more frequently with abstract words. Specifically, Naumann et al. (2018) performed their analyses across parts-of-speech by comparing the behaviour of nouns, verbs and adjectives in large-scale corpora. These results are not fully in line with various theories of cognition which suggest that both concrete and abstract words should co-occur more often with concrete words because concrete information links the real-world usage of both concrete and abstract words to their mental representation (Barsalou, 1999; Pecher et al., 2011).

2 The Current Study

In the current study we build on prior evidence from the literature and perform a more fine-grained corpus-based analysis on the distribution of concrete and abstract words by specifically looking at the types of syntactic relations that connect nouns to verbs in sentences. More specifically, we look at the concreteness of verbs and the corresponding nouns as subjects, direct objects and prepositional objects. This study is carried out in a quantitative fashion to identify general trends. However, we also look into specific examples to better understand the types of nouns that attach to specific verbs.

First of all, we expect to replicate the main results from Naumann et al. (2018): in general, concrete nouns should co-occur more frequently with concrete verbs and abstract nouns with abstract verbs. Moreover, we expect to identify the main patterns that characterise semantic effects of an interaction of concreteness in verb-noun subcategorisation, such as collocations and meaning shifts.

The motivation for this study is twofold: (1) From a cognitive science perspective we seek additional and more fine-grained evidence to better understand the clash between the existing corpus-based studies and the theories of cognition which predict predominantly concrete information in the context of both concrete and abstract words. (2) From a computational perspective we expect some variability in the interaction of concreteness in verb-noun subcategorisation, given that abstract contexts are ubiquitous and salient empirical indicators for non-literal language identification, cf. *carry a bag* vs. *carry a risk.*

3   Materials

In the following analyses, we used nouns and verbs extracted from the Brysbaert et al. (2014) collection of concreteness ratings. In this resource, the concreteness of 40,000 English words was evaluated by human participants on a scale from 1 (abstract) to 5 (concrete).

Given that participants did not have any overt information about part-of-speech (henceforth, POS) while performing the norming study, Brysbaert et al. added this information post-hoc from the SUBTLEX-US, a 51-million word subtitle corpus (Brysbaert and New, 2009). In order to align the POS information to the current study, we disambiguated the POS of the normed words by extracting their most frequent POS from the 10-billion word corpus ENCOW16AX (see below for details). Moreover, as discussed in previous studies by Naumann et al. (2018) and Pollock (2018), mid-range concreteness scores indicate words that are difficult to categorise unambiguously regarding their concreteness. For this reason and in order to obtain a clear picture of the behaviour of concrete vs. abstract words, we selected only words with very high (concrete) or very low (abstract) concreteness scores. We included in our analyses the 1000 most concrete (concreteness range: 4.86 – 5.00) and 1000 most abstract (1.04 – 1.76) nouns, and the 500 most concrete (3.80 – 5.00) and most abstract (1.19 – 2.00) verbs. We chose to include a smaller selection of verbs compared to the nouns because we considered verbs to be more difficult to evaluate by humans according to their concreteness scores and consequently noisier and more ambiguous for the analyses we are conducting.

The corpus analyses were performed on the parsed version of the sentence-shuffled English ENCOW16AX corpus (Schäfer and Bildhauer, 2012). For each sentence in the corpus, we extracted the verbs in combination with the nouns when they both occur in our selection of words from Brysbaert et al. (2014) and when the nouns are parsed as subjects (in active and passive sentences: *nsubj* and *nsubjpass*), direct objects (*dobj*) or prepositional objects (*pobj*) of the verbs. In the case of *pobj*, we considered the 20 most frequent prepositions (e.g., *of, in, for, at*) in the corpus.

In total, we extracted 11,716,189 verb-noun token pairs including 3,814,048 abstract verb tokens; 7,902,141 concrete verb tokens; 3,701,669 abstract noun tokens; and 8,014,520 concrete noun tokens. In 2,958,308 cases, the noun was parsed as the subject of the verb (with 748,438 of them as subjects in passive constructions), in 5,011,347 cases the noun was the direct object, and in 3,746,534 cases the noun was a prepositional object. Already by looking at these numbers it is possible to identify a strong frequency bias in favour of concrete words; we will discuss later in the paper how this bias affects the results reported. All the analyses reported in the following sections are performed at token level.

4   Quantitative Analysis

In a pre-test we analysed the overall distributions of verbs and nouns according to their concreteness scores. Figure 1 shows the overall distributions of verbs (left, M=3.4, SD=1.1) and nouns (right, M=3.9, SD=1.6) included in our analyses. Overall, nouns have significantly more extreme values than verbs: the majority of concrete nouns have concreteness scores clustering around 5.00 while concrete verbs cluster around 4.0. Similarly, abstract nouns have significantly lower scores (i.e., they are more abstract) than

Function	Abstract Verbs	Concrete Verbs	Difference C-A	Overall
nsubj	3.57 ($\pm$ 1.65)	4.41 ($\pm$ 1.22)	0.84***	4.07 ($\pm$ 1.46)
nsubjpass	3.34 ($\pm$ 1.68)	4.20 ($\pm$ 1.39)	0.86***	3.85 ($\pm$ 1.56)
dobj	2.65 ($\pm$ 1.58)	4.30 ($\pm$ 1.31)	1.65***	3.76 ($\pm$ 1.60)
pobj	3.10 ($\pm$ 1.66)	4.20 ($\pm$ 1.38)	1.10***	3.91 ($\pm$ 1.54)
in	3.06 ($\pm$ 1.65)	4.37 ($\pm$ 1.25)	1.31***	4.01 ($\pm$ 1.49)
at	2.58 ($\pm$ 1.51)	4.11 ($\pm$ 1.24)	1.53***	3.79 ($\pm$ 1.58)
for	2.86 ($\pm$ 1.64)	3.36 ($\pm$ 1.69)	0.50***	3.15 ($\pm$ 1.69)
of	3.21 ($\pm$ 1.67)	4.23 ($\pm$ 1.36)	1.02***	3.92 ($\pm$ 1.53)

Table 1: Mean concreteness scores ($\pm$ standard deviation) and differences between the nouns subcategorised by concrete vs. abstract verbs within a specific syntactic function.

abstract verbs. The numerical difference in the presence of extreme scores is also highlighted by the much higher standard deviation characterising nouns compared to verbs. We interpret the lower amount of "real" extremes (1 and 5) for verbs as an indicator of the difficulty that participants had to clearly norm verbs compared to nouns. For example, while comparing the nouns *belief*$_{1.2}$ and *ball*$_{5.0}$ humans would have a clear agreement on highly abstract and highly concrete scores; on the contrary, the distinction between *moralise*$_{1.4}$ and *sit*$_{4.8}$ might be less clear.[1]

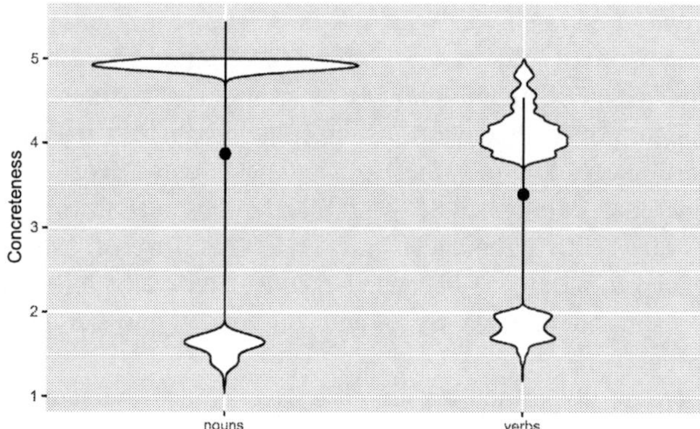

Figure 1: Overall distribution of concreteness scores for nouns (left) and verbs (right). The dots indicate the mean values and the solid vertical lines mark the standard deviations.

In our main study, we analysed the concreteness of the nouns that are in a specific and direct syntactic relation with verbs. The overall distributions in Figure 2 are extremely consistent across syntactic relations: when looking at the means, the concreteness of nouns subcategorised by concrete verbs is significantly higher than the concreteness of nouns subcategorised by abstract verbs (all p-values < 0.001). This result is perfectly in line with the more general analysis by Naumann et al. (2018).

Table 1 investigates more deeply the interaction between the concreteness of verbs and nouns for different syntactic functions. It reports the average concreteness scores of the nouns subcategorised by concrete and abstract verbs ($\pm$ standard deviation), the difference between the concrete and abstract scores (with significance tests) and the overall average concreteness score by function. The statistical analyses have been performed using a standard linear regression model. The comparison between the scores in the first two columns (Abstract Verbs and Concrete Verbs) confirms that subject and direct object nouns that are subcategorised by concrete verbs are significantly more concrete than those subcategorised by abstract verbs. The "Difference C-A" column shows that these differences are all highly significant. In addition, the nouns subcategorised by concrete verbs are extremely high on the concreteness scale (mean

---

[1]In this paper the number in subscript indicates the concreteness score from the Brysbaert et al. (2014) norms.

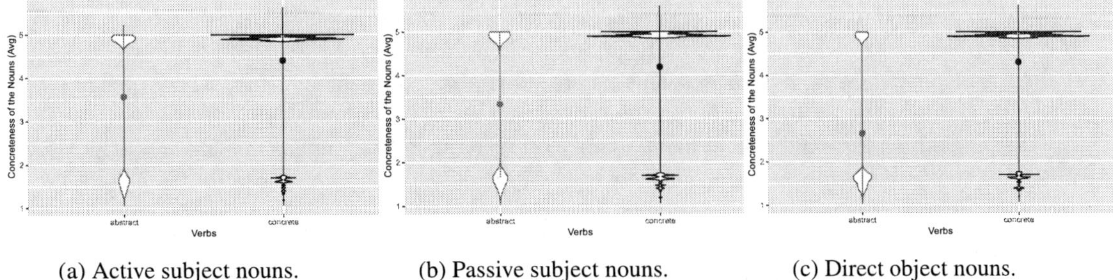

(a) Active subject nouns.   (b) Passive subject nouns.   (c) Direct object nouns.

Figure 2: Distribution of concreteness scores for the nouns subcategorised by abstract (left/red) and concrete (right/blue) verbs in different syntactic functions. The dots indicate the mean values and the solid vertical lines mark the standard deviations.

values: $4.2 - 4.41$) while the nouns subcategorised by abstract verbs have only mid-scores (mean values: $2.65 - 3.57$).

By zooming in on the specific functions, we see that subjects are significantly more concrete than direct objects for both abstract and concrete verbs. The concreteness scores of subjects of passivised sentences are in between in both categories. This pattern is confirmed by looking at the "Overall" column.

Prepositional objects that are subcategorised by concrete verbs are significantly more concrete than prepositional objects subcategorised by abstract verbs, across prepositions. However, given the extreme variability in the prepositions used, we will analyse the most representative *pobjs* more specifically in the following section.

5   Qualitative Analysis

In order to better understand the patterns of concreteness behind each syntactic function introduced in the previous section, we performed a series of qualitative analyses, by looking at the most frequent verb-noun combinations grouped by syntactic function. For both functions *nsubj* and *dobj* we see the same strong pattern as in the general analyses in Section 4: concrete verbs have a strong overall preference for concrete complements ($map_{4.9}$ $show_{4.0}$, $boil_{4.2}$ $water_{5.0}$). Regarding abstract verbs, we find a preference for subcategorising abstract direct objects ($reduce_{2.0}$ $risk_{1.6}$), but -in contrast- a preference for concrete subjects ($student_{4.9}$ $need_{1.7}$). Appropriately, surface subjects in passivised clauses have preferences that are in between those for surface subjects and direct objects in active clauses, presumably because they are semantically comparable to the direct objects of the action encoded by the corresponding verb.

When looking into exceptions to this predominant pattern, we find collocations and non-literal language, such as metaphors and metonyms. For example, metaphorical language usage occurs when concrete verbs attach to abstract direct objects ($carry_{4.0}$ $risk_{1.6}$ vs. $carry_{4.0}$ $bag_{4.9}$, $catch_{4.1}$ $moment_{1.6}$ vs. $catch_{4.1}$ $insect_{4.9}$); while abstract verbs collocated with concrete direct objects trigger a metonymical use ($recommend_{1.7}$ $book_{4.9}$ vs. $write_{4.2}$ $book_{4.9}$).

When looking at prepositional objects it is possible to identify three main behaviours: i) a main preference for concrete verbs and nouns (e.g., "in" and "at"); ii) a strong interaction with abstract verbs and nouns (e.g., "for"); iii) a mixed co-occurrence with both concrete and abstract verbs and nouns (e.g.,"of"). The following paragraphs report a qualitative discussion about the predominant verbs and nouns with regard to the four prepositions "in", "at", "for", and "of".

The preposition *in* manifests a very strong interaction with concrete verbs and concrete nouns. Some examples among the most frequent ones in the corpus are: $write_{4.2}$ *in* $book_{4.9}$ and $sleep_{4.4}$ *in* $bed_{5.0}$. The only rare exceptions to this pattern refer to idiomatic structures like: $carry_{4.0}$ *in* $accordance_{1.5}$ or $carry_{4.0}$ *in* $manner_{1.6}$. Table 1 confirms that the preposition *in* triggers very high concreteness scores in general and the highest concreteness scores for nouns that are subcategorised by concrete verbs.

The preposition *at* connects mainly concrete verbs with concrete nouns: *sit*$_{4.8}$ *at table*$_{4.9}$ and *eat*$_{4.4}$ *at restaurant*$_{4.9}$. However, in strong collocations it shows a preference for abstract nouns: *jump*$_{4.5}$ *at chance*$_{1.6}$ or *happen*$_{1.8}$ *at moment*$_{1.6}$. This pattern is confirmed by Table 1 too, where concrete verbs have high scores while abstract verbs have the lowest scores in the entire table.

The preposition *for*, on the other hand, mainly occurs with abstract nouns that are subcategorised by abstract verbs: *need*$_{1.7}$ *for purpose*$_{1.5}$ and *imagine*$_{1.5}$ *for moment*$_{1.6}$. Exceptions to this pattern are due to metonymic readings like *write*$_{4.2}$ *for magazine*$_{5.0}$ and *run*$_{4.3}$ *for office*$_{4.9}$. Correspondingly, we see the lowest overall concreteness score across verbs in Table 1.

Finally, the preposition *of* shows a mixed interaction in the concreteness of verbs and nouns. This preposition co-occurs mainly with very concrete verbs that however subcategorise both highly concrete nouns (*run*$_{4.3}$ *of water*$_5$) but also highly abstract nouns (*run*$_{4.3}$ *of idea*$_{1.6}$) in cases of metaphorical use. As expected, the overall concreteness for this function in Table 1 is among the highest both for concrete and abstract verbs.

6 General Discussion & Conclusion

The aim of this study was to provide a fine-grained empirical analysis of the concreteness nature in verb-noun subcategorisation. The general pattern already described in Naumann et al. (2018) is confirmed by our quantitative analysis: overall, concrete verbs predominantly subcategorise concrete nouns as subjects and direct objects, while abstract verbs predominantly subcategorise abstract nouns as subjects and direct objects. A qualitative analysis revealed that exceptions to the predominant same-class interaction indicate semantic effects in verb-noun interaction: collocation, metaphor and metonymy, which shows the usefulness of detecting abstractness in the contexts of verbs as salient features in automatic non-literal language identification.

A slightly more variable pattern emerges when looking at prepositional objects. We identified three main clusters of prepositions that behave differently according to their preferred nouns and verbs. The prepositions in the first cluster (e.g., "in" and "at") co-occur mostly with concrete verbs and nouns; the prepositions in the second cluster (e.g., "for") have a strong preference for abstract verbs and nouns; while the prepositions in the third cluster (e.g, "of") show variability in the concreteness of the related nouns. Once again, the divergence form the general pattern is often ascribable to cases of non-literal language.

This study, on the one hand, provided additional and more fine-grained evidence of the clash between the existing corpus-based studies and the theories of cognition which predict predominantly concrete information in the context of both concrete and abstract words. This was achieved by zooming in on the contexts which stand in a direct syntactic relation to the target word. In addition, they provided useful indicators to the implementation of computational models for the automatic identification and classification of non-literal language.

References

Aedmaa, E., M. Köper, and S. Schulte im Walde (2018). Combining Abstractness and Language-specific Theoretical Indicators for Detecting Non-Literal Usage of Estonian Particle Verbs. In *Proceedings of the NAACL 2018 Student Research Workshop*, New Orleans, LA, USA, pp. 9–16.

Barsalou, L. W. (1999). Perceptual Symbol Systems. *Behavioral and Brain Sciences 22*, 577–660.

Barsalou, L. W. and K. Wiemer-Hastings (2005). Situating Abstract Concepts. In D. Pecher and R. Zwaan (Eds.), *Grounding Cognition: The Role of Perception and Action in Memory, Language, and Thinking*, Chapter 7, pp. 129–163. New York: Cambridge University Press.

Bhaskar, S. A., M. Köper, S. Schulte im Walde, and D. Frassinelli (2017). Exploring Multi-Modal Text+Image Models to Distinguish between Abstract and Concrete Nouns. In *Proceedings of the IWCS Workshop on Foundations of Situated and Multimodal Communication*, Montpellier, France.

Brysbaert, M. and B. New (2009). Moving beyond Kučera and Francis: A Critical Evaluation of Current Word Frequency Norms and the Introduction of a New and Improved Word Frequency Measure for American English. *Behavior Research Methods 41*(4), 977–990.

Brysbaert, M., A. B. Warriner, and V. Kuperman (2014). Concreteness Ratings for 40 Thousand generally known English Word Lemmas. *Behavior Research Methods 64*, 904–911.

Frassinelli, D., D. Naumann, J. Utt, and S. Schulte im Walde (2017). Contextual Characteristics of Concrete and Abstract Words. In *Proceedings of the 12th International Conference on Computational Semantics*, Montpellier, France.

Hill, F., A. Korhonen, and C. Bentz (2014). A Quantitative Empirical Analysis of the Abstract/Concrete Distinction. *Cognitive Science 38*(1), 162–177.

Köper, M. and S. Schulte im Walde (2016). Distinguishing Literal and Non-Literal Usage of German Particle Verbs. In *Proceedings of the Conference of the North American Chapter of the Association for Computational Linguistics: Human Language Technologies*, San Diego, California, USA, pp. 353–362.

McRae, K. and M. Jones (2013). Semantic Memory. *The Oxford Handbook of Cognitive Psychology 206*.

Naumann, D., D. Frassinelli, and S. Schulte im Walde (2018). Quantitative Semantic Variation in the Contexts of Concrete and Abstract Words. In *Proceedings of the 7th Joint Conference on Lexical and Computational Semantics*, New Orleans, LA, USA, pp. 76–85.

Pecher, D., I. Boot, and S. Van Dantzig (2011). Abstract Concepts. Sensory-Motor Grounding, Metaphors, and Beyond. *Psychology of Learning and Motivation – Advances in Research and Theory 54*, 217–248.

Pollock, L. (2018). Statistical and Methodological Problems with Concreteness and other Semantic Variables: A List Memory Experiment Case Study. *Behavior Research Methods 50*(3), 1198–1216.

Schäfer, R. and F. Bildhauer (2012). Building Large Corpora from the Web Using a New Efficient Tool Chain. In *Proceedings of the 8th International Conference on Language Resources and Evaluation*, Istanbul, Turkey, pp. 486–493.

Turney, P., Y. Neuman, D. Assaf, and Y. Cohen (2011). Literal and Metaphorical Sense Identification through Concrete and Abstract Context. In *Proceedings of the Conference on Empirical Methods in Natural Language Processing*, Edinburgh, UK, pp. 680–690.

Vigliocco, G., S.-T. Kousta, P. A. Della Rosa, D. P. Vinson, M. Tettamanti, J. T. Devlin, and S. F. Cappa (2014). The Neural Representation of Abstract Words: The Role of Emotion. *Cerebral Cortex 24*(7), 1767–1777.

Generating a Novel Dataset of Multimodal Referring Expressions

Nikhil Krishnaswamy
Brandeis University
nkrishna@brandeis.edu

James Pustejovsky
Brandeis University
jamesp@brandeis.edu

Abstract

Referring expressions and definite descriptions of objects in space exploit information about both object characteristics and locations. Linguistic referencing strategies can rely on increasingly high-level abstractions to distinguish an object in a given location from similar ones elsewhere, yet the description of the intended location may still be unnatural or difficult to interpret. Modalities like gesture may communicate spatial information like locations in a more concise manner. When communicating with each other, humans mix language and gesture to reference entities, changing modalities as needed. Recent progress in AI and human-computer interaction has created systems where a human can interact with a computer multimodally, but computers often lack the capacity to intelligently mix modalities when generating referring expressions. We present a novel dataset of referring expressions combining natural language and gesture, describe its creation and evaluation, and its uses to train models for generating and interpreting multimodal referring expressions.

1 Introduction

Psychological studies suggest that gesture serves as a bridge between understanding actions situated in the world and linguistic descriptions, such as symbolic references to entity classes and attributes (Butterworth, 2003; Capirci et al., 2005). Many researchers (e.g., Clark et al. (1983); Volterra et al. (2005)), view gesture as a common mode of reference vis-à-vis *common ground*. Gesture is well-suited to directly grounding spatial information; pointing can bind to a location or be coerced to object(s) in that location (Ballard et al., 1997). Demonstrative or attributive language (e.g., size, shape, qualitative relations), can specify entities by binding those characteristics to information received via gesture. Thus, language affords abstract strategies to distinguish an object in a given location from similar ones elsewhere (e.g., *the chair closest to that door*—with pointing, or *the green block at the right side of the table*).

As an environment becomes more complex, so does the language used to give directions or single out specific items in it (Skubic et al., 2004; Moratz and Tenbrink, 2006). An object indicated by deixis is usually also the topic of discussion (Brooks and Breazeal, 2006), but deixis may be ambiguous depending on distance from agent to target object, or other objects close to the target object (Latoschik and Wachsmuth, 1997), while language can supplement it for more useful definite descriptions (Bangerter, 2004). Co-temporal/overlapping speech and gesture (or an "ensemble" (Pustejovsky, 2018)) often involves deixis to ground the location, and language to specify further information (Sluis and Krahmer, 2004). As a task's natural language requirements grow more complex, subjects rely on other modalities to carry semantic load, particularly as the need for immediate interpretation grows (Whitney et al., 2016).

Studies in this area have a long history in computational linguistics/semantics (e.g., Claassen (1992); Krahmer and van der Sluis (2003)), human-robot interaction (e.g., Kelleher and Kruijff (2006); Foster et al. (2008)), and computational and human discourse studies (e.g., Bortfeld and Brennan (1997); Funakoshi et al. (2004); Viethen and Dale (2008)). Following these, we seek to build models for generating, recognizing, and classifying referring expressions that are both *natural* and *useful* to the human interlocutors of computational dialogue systems. Here, we present a novel dataset of Embodied Multimodal Referring Expressions (EMRE), blending gesture and natural language (English text-to-speech), used by an avatar in a human-computer interaction (HCI) scenario. We describe raw data generation, annotation and evaluation, preliminary analysis, and expected uses in training machine learning models for generating referring expressions in real-time that are appropriate, salient, and natural in context.

2 Data Gathering

As our goal is to train models which a system can use to generate and interpret naturalistic multimodal referring expressions during interaction with a human, we gathered data using such a system—specifically VoxSim, a semantically-driven visual event simulator based on the VoxML semantic modeling language (Pustejovsky and Krishnaswamy, 2016), that facilitates data gathering using Monte-Carlo parameter setting to simulate motion predicates in 3D space (Krishnaswamy and Pustejovsky, 2016). We created a variant on the *Human-Avatar-Blocks World* (HAB) system (Krishnaswamy et al., 2017; Narayana et al., 2018), in which VoxSim visualizes the actions taken by an avatar in the 3D world as she interprets gestural and spoken input from a human interlocutor.[1] A shortcoming of the HAB system is the asymmetry between the language that the system's avatar is capable of recognizing and interpreting, and the English utterances it can generate (Krishnaswamy and Pustejovsky, 2018). Specifically, the avatar can 1) produce complete sentences of structures that it cannot entirely parse and 2) properly interpret spatial terms and relations between objects, but cannot fluently use them to refer to objects or the relations between them. Improvements to the first asymmetry are under development separately, and here we present data for creating a robust model of referring techniques in all available modalities, to help rectify the second asymmetry, for more fluent interaction in this and other HCI systems.

The gesture semantics in VoxSim are largely based on the formalisms of Lascarides and Stone (2006; 2009a; 2009b). Multimodal information in a multimodal system cannot be assumed to follow the same format as unimodal information (Oviatt, 1999). Language in an ensemble cannot be assumed to be identical to language used alone. A reference to an object may be grounded in gesture, natural language, or both, subject to constraints that vary per modality. We therefore generated a dataset that can be examined for where these

$$
\textbf{point} \begin{bmatrix} \text{TYPE} = \begin{bmatrix} \text{HEAD} = \textbf{assignment} \\ \text{ARGS} = \begin{bmatrix} A_1 = \textbf{x:agent} \\ A_2 = \textbf{y:finger} \\ A_3 = \textbf{z:location} \\ A_4 = \textbf{w:physobj}\bullet\textbf{location} \end{bmatrix} \\ \text{BODY} = \begin{bmatrix} E_1 = extend(x,y) \\ E_2 = def(vec(x \rightarrow y \times z), as(w)) \end{bmatrix} \end{bmatrix} \end{bmatrix}
$$

Figure 1: VoxML typing of [[POINT]] (Pustejovsky and Krishnaswamy, 2016). E_2 defines the target of deixis as the intersection of the vector extended in e_1 with a location, and reifies that point as a variable w. A_4, shows the compound binding of w to the indicated region and objects within that region.

constraints occur, and under which circumstances human evaluators, as proxies for interlocutors with the avatar in a live interaction, prefer one referring modality to another, and with what descriptive detail.

2.1 Video and Quantitative Data

In our test scenario, there are six equally-sized target blocks on a table, for which the avatar generates referring expressions; two each are *red*, *green*, or *purple*. This gives each block an identifiable, non-unique characteristic that requires disambiguation. They may also be used in the definite descriptions of other blocks. There are three unique objects on the table: a *plate*, a *knife*, and a *cup*. These "landmark" objects will never be the object of a referring expression, but may be used in referring to the target block.

In all scenes, we store the spatial relations between all objects. We used qualitative relations as defined in a subset of the Region Connection Calculus (RCC8) (Randell et al., 1992) and Ternary Point Configuration Calculus (TPCC) (Moratz et al., 2002), and included in the library QSRLib (Gatsoulis et al., 2016). Where calculi in QSRLib only cover 2D spatial relations, VoxSim uses extensions such as RCC-3D (Albath et al., 2010) or computes axial overlap with the Separating Hyperplane Theorem (Schneider, 2014). All spatial relations used were mapped to a linguistic term, such that the RCC8 relation *EC* (*E*xternally *C*onnected) would be referred to as *touching* in the language generation phase.

For generating utterances, we explore 2 variables: number of relational adjuncts, and type of demonstratives used. Conditions on proximal vs. distal demonstratives have been explored in multiple studies (Botley and McEnery, 2001; Strauss, 2002) and the boundaries between proximal and distal egocentric

---

[1] https://github.com/VoxML/VoxSim

space are regularly shown to be flexible (Coventry et al., 2014). The distributions of demonstratives vary across languages (Proulx, 1988; Meira, 2003; Hayashi, 2004; Piwek et al., 2008) but seem to be consistently conditioned on distance (spatial, textual, or grammatical) between all indexes involved in an utterance and not just the object of focus. This data is only for English definite descriptions but VoxSim provides a platform to create multimodally grounded data for any language, in principle.

This data comprises a set of approximately 10-second videos, each showing the avatar referring to one object. Blocks and landmark objects were placed randomly in the scene, and each block was referred to in turn. All videos consist of two segments: **1**) The target object is encircled in pink to draw attention to it; **2**) the avatar indicates the target object with either an animated deictic gesture (pointing), with spoken English, or an ensemble containing both. The camera through which the 3D virtual world is rendered is placed at the coordinates of the avatar's head, so directions in her linguistic descriptions are consistent with the viewer's perspective. *In front of* x means closer to the agent than x and *behind* x is further away. The avatar referred to each object five times: once with gesture only, twice with spoken language only, and twice with the ensemble. Where gesture was involved, the avatar pointed to the object with the closer hand as measured by Euclidean distance, with an extended index finger (see Fig. 2). The extended finger (the *stroke phase* per Kendon (2004)) was held for 2 seconds.

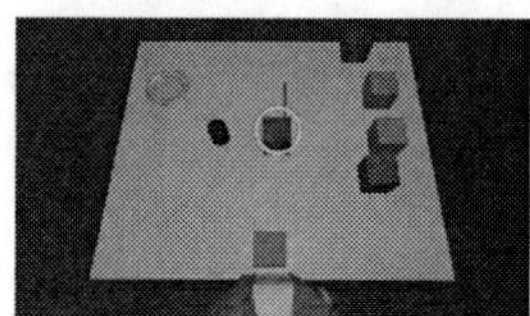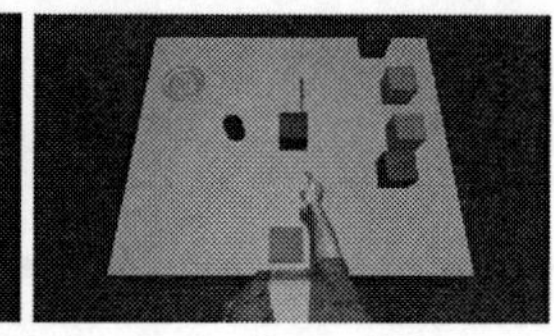

Figure 2: Sample frames. The pink circle (L) indicates the red block in the center as the target object. (R) shows the avatar pointing to it. The block might be described as "this red block" or "that red block in front of the knife", or, without deixis, "the red block right of the cup" or "the red block in front of the knife, right of the cup, and left of the green block."

We generated linguistic descriptions using the following process: **1**) If the referring modality was solely linguistic, the article "the" was used. For ensembles, a demonstrative "that" or "this" was used, and use of a distance distinction was randomly `false`—where the demonstrative was always "that"—or `true`. If `true`, the distinction type was randomly **relative** or **absolute**. For a *relative* distinction, "this" object was the closer of two identically-colored blocks to the agent, and "that" was the further of the two. For *absolute*, "this" was any object in the half of the table closer to the agent, and "that," any object in the other half. **2**) A set of n (randomly selected $\in \{0..3\}$) relational descriptors were constructed describing the target object's current relations to other objects, ordered randomly. See Fig. 2 for multiple ways of describing a target object.

Each of the 6 blocks was referred to in turn, after which the objects on the table were moved to new random locations, and references started over. We captured 50 different object configurations, for a total of 1,500 video object references (5 references × 6 blocks × 50 configurations).[2] For each video, the referring modality, distance distinction and type, full descriptive phrase if any, and relational descriptors were stored in a database, with the full set of all object coordinates in the configuration depicted, the full relation set describing the configuration, and the Euclidean distance from the target object to the agent.

2.2 Annotation

Videos, grouped by configuration, were posted to Amazon Mechanical Turk (MTurk) as Human Intelligence Tasks (HITs). Each HIT contained the 5 videos showing references to one target in one configuration, and was completed by 8 Workers, for a total of 2,400 HITs. Workers were paid $0.10 per HIT and were given a maximum of 30 minutes to complete each. Each Worker viewed the 5 videos and ranked them on a Likert-type scale by how *natural* they considered the reference method in the video, 1 being least natural and 5 most. Workers could optionally add how they would have made definite reference to the target object. If Workers ranked the videos 1-2-3-4-5 or 5-4-3-2-1, we asked them to textually confirm this intent, to limit bots or workers not actually performing the task. We rejected answers that tied more than three videos, to limit bots or workers automatically ranking all the same. This process resulted in 1,500 videos depicting referring methods for objects in various configurations with quantitative values

---

[2]A sample video can be viewed at https://s3.amazonaws.com/emre-videos/emre_vid/EMRE-2019-01-07-095844.mp4

describing each, and 2,228 assessments of the naturalness of procedurally-generated references. Of the 2,400 HITs, 172 were rejected for not following instructions (providing rankings outside the 1-5 range or using non-numerical values), or for being judged as trying to game the system.[3] Workers on this task were limited to English speakers, and had an average lifetime approval rate of 93.25%. Over the entire batch, Workers took an average of 12 minutes, 11.5 seconds to complete each HIT.

3 Analysis and Discussion

We analyzed the probability distributions of typically high- and low-ranked referring expressions relative to various conditions in the video containing them. For instance, if "ensemble" referring expressions have a higher probability of a high rank than purely gestural references, this would demonstrate evaluators' preference for them. If, however, ensemble referring expressions are only more likely to receive a high ranking compared to gestural references when the target object is far from the agent, this would suggest that distance is a factor in using language to disambiguate. Since we used a Likert-type scale to rank the videos, leading to the possibility that evaluators would rank all videos as relatively good or bad but some better/worse than others, we not only assessed the probability of a video generated under a certain set of conditions receiving a particular score 1–5, but also the probability of a video receiving a score worse/better (± 2) than the median score of all that evaluator's rankings on that individual task. Below we present some of the strongest predictors and most interesting dependencies uncovered.

Fig. 3 shows the relative probability of score conditioned on *modality*. It is very clear that there is a strong preference for the *ensemble* (in yellow) compared to the others, and that the gesture only method (in blue) was routinely ranked worst while language only was more likely average in terms of naturalness. From the graph on the right, we can see that while the ensemble method was still most likely to achieve ratings above the median, this was not always *far* (i.e., +2) above the median, suggesting that either most referencing methods were considered adequate (the percentages at $X = 0$ also suggest this), or the ensemble method itself could be bettered in some way (likely by clearer or more detailed language—see Fig. 5). This indicates that while language alone suffices for definite reference but leaves room for improvement, and gesture alone is often insufficient, the combination is usually more natural, perhaps due to semantic content that is redundant in context and further reduces ambiguity (Gatt et al., 2011).

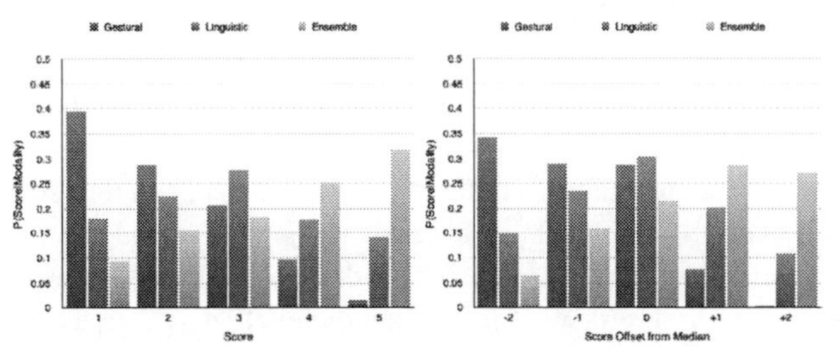

Figure 3: $P(\text{Score}|\text{Modality})$ [L]; $P(\text{Diff from median}|\text{Modality})$ [R]

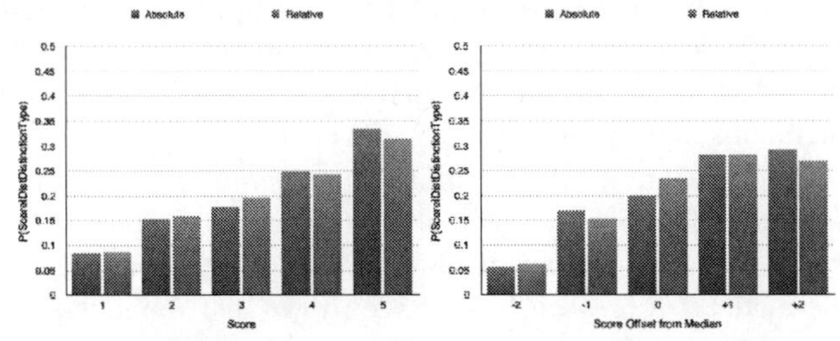

Figure 4: $P(\text{Score}|\text{Dist. distinction type})$ [L]; $P(\text{Diff from median}|\text{Dist. distinction type})$ [R]

Fig. 4 shows the probability of a referring method (in the *ensemble* modality only) receiving a score given the type of distance distinction used. The *absolute* distance distinction (shown in blue), is somewhat more likely than the *relative* distinction type to score highly suggesting either a relatively static demarcation between points considered "proximal" to the agent and "distal" points, or some role for the table, the surface relative to which the distance distinction was calculated. Conditioning on distance from object to agent showed no significant difference in probabilities.

Fig. 5 shows the probability of a particular rank given the number of relational descriptors used, for

---

[3]Some initial rejections on the basis of gaming the system were reversed upon subsequent communication with the worker, and these were included in the 2,228 figure.

the linguistic (L) and ensemble (R) modalities. In all cases evaluators slightly preferred 3 descriptors, and often 1 descriptor over 2 in the ensemble modality. This suggests something of a conflict between a clear if unwieldy use of 3 descriptors, and a concise single descriptor used with gesture.

Many more parameters can be analyzed for dependencies, and we have released evaluation scripts along with along with the fully-annotated dataset.[4] These initial results show clear preference for the ensemble referring method, a slight preference for absolute distance distinction as opposed to relative, and for more relational descriptors used in ensemble with gesture. We will also examine the data for dependencies be-

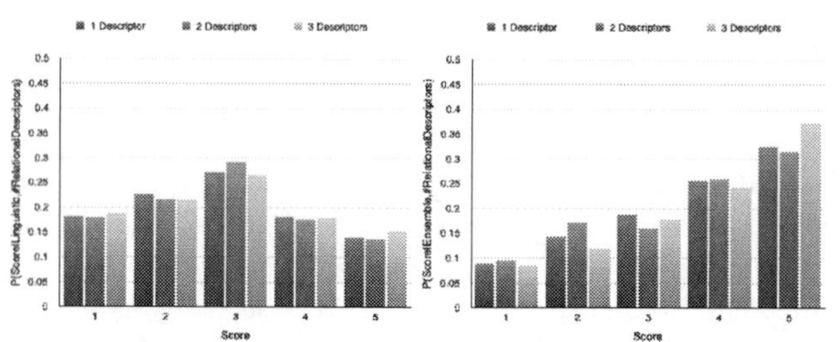

Figure 5: $P(\text{Score}|\text{Language only, \# Descriptors})$ [L]; $P(\text{Score}|\text{Ensemble, \# Descriptors})$ [R]

tween preference for number of descriptors, or distance from the agent to the target object, and the total set of relations in the scene. Modeling these will allow better ability to assess the entire scene context when generating natural referring expressions.

4 Conclusions and Future Work

Early analysis shows that evaluators, as a proxy for the human interlocutor, perceive references using the gesture-speech *ensemble* as more natural than unimodal referring methods. Not only does this make a convincing case for the computer to incorporate gestural output for fluent HCI, but we have also uncovered circumstances under which humans are likely to perceive the computer as referring fluently and naturally to objects in the interaction. The strongest predictor of high naturalness is the expressive modality, but there are many dependencies and we have provided techniques for uncovering those.

Going forward, we seek to use the evaluated data to train a model that can be deployed within this and other HCI systems to generate natural multimodal referring expressions in real-time, and to not only capture the strong predictors from Sec. 3, but also more subtle dependencies between contextual parameters. Some technical issues and solutions we anticipate are: **1)** Dependencies between multiple paramaters may arise from a particular configuration (e.g., two similar objects close to each other but too far from the agent to distinguish with deixis) that requires choosing a modality or level of specificity at runtime. We would suggest a convolutional neural net approach to assess relations in the scene, with gradients weighted by the information gained or lost by the addition of a particular relational descriptor for the target object; **2)** There may be cases when the avatar cannot use her hands for deixis (e.g., while holding other objects)—in this case she would need an intelligent model of linguistic-only reference to adequately single out an object in context; **3)** To capture the context of prior actions (e.g., *the green block next to the red block I just put down*), we would recommend a sequential model trained on the object configuration relation sets in the EMRE dataset, with an Approximate Nearest Neighbor (ANN) classifier between configurations in a live interaction and configurations in the data.

We have presented a novel dataset of referring techniques for definite objects in multiple configurations, with a goal of varying and combining multiple modalities available in a human-computer interaction system. As the dataset is relatively small, it should be expanded and linked to other multimodal corpora before training a publicly-deployable model, but previously we have shown that simulated data using qualitative relations is suitable for learning over smaller sample sizes (Krishnaswamy et al., 2019), and so we believe it is appropriate for training an initial model. Data like this should be of great use to researchers developing intelligent referring strategies in multimodal systems and to researchers studying multimodal semantics and referring expressions in general. After analysis, we have proposed some techniques for training models for its reuse and are currently developing experiments in which to deploy them.

---

[4]https://github.com/VoxML/public-data/tree/master/EMRE/HIT

References

Albath, J., J. L. Leopold, C. L. Sabharwal, and A. M. Maglia (2010). RCC-3D: Qualitative spatial reasoning in 3D. In *CAINE*, pp. 74–79.

Ballard, D. H., M. M. Hayhoe, P. K. Pook, and R. P. Rao (1997). Deictic codes for the embodiment of cognition. *Behavioral and Brain Sciences 20*(4), 723–742.

Bangerter, A. (2004). Using pointing and describing to achieve joint focus of attention in dialogue. *Psychological Science 15*(6), 415–419.

Bortfeld, H. and S. E. Brennan (1997). Use and acquisition of idiomatic expressions in referring by native and non-native speakers. *Discourse Processes 23*(2), 119–147.

Botley, S. and T. McEnery (2001). Proximal and distal demonstratives: A corpus-based study. *Journal of English Linguistics 29*(3), 214–233.

Brooks, A. G. and C. Breazeal (2006). Working with robots and objects: Revisiting deictic reference for achieving spatial common ground. In *Proceedings of the 1st ACM SIGCHI/SIGART conference on Human-robot interaction*, pp. 297–304. ACM.

Butterworth, G. (2003). Pointing is the royal road to language for babies. In *Pointing*, pp. 17–42. Psychology Press.

Capirci, O., A. Contaldo, M. C. Caselli, and V. Volterra (2005). From action to language through gesture: A longitudinal perspective. *Gesture 5*(1), 155–177.

Claassen, W. (1992). Generating referring expressions in a multimodal environment. In *Aspects of automated natural language generation*, pp. 247–262. Springer.

Clark, H. H., R. Schreuder, and S. Buttrick (1983). Common ground at the understanding of demonstrative reference. *Journal of verbal learning and verbal behavior 22*(2), 245–258.

Coventry, K. R., D. Griffiths, and C. J. Hamilton (2014). Spatial demonstratives and perceptual space: Describing and remembering object location. *Cognitive Psychology 69*, 46–70.

Foster, M. E., E. G. Bard, M. Guhe, R. L. Hill, J. Oberlander, and A. Knoll (2008). The roles of haptic-ostensive referring expressions in cooperative, task-based human-robot dialogue. In *Proceedings of the 3rd ACM/IEEE international conference on Human robot interaction*, pp. 295–302. ACM.

Funakoshi, K., S. Watanabe, N. Kuriyama, and T. Tokunaga (2004). Generating referring expressions using perceptual groups. In *International Conference on Natural Language Generation*, pp. 51–60. Springer.

Gatsoulis, Y., M. Alomari, C. Burbridge, C. Dondrup, P. Duckworth, P. Lightbody, M. Hanheide, N. Hawes, D. Hogg, A. Cohn, et al. (2016). Qsrlib: a software library for online acquisition of qualitative spatial relations from video.

Gatt, A., R. van Gompel, E. Krahmer, and K. van Deemter (2011). Non-deterministic attribute selection in reference production. In *Proceedings of the 2nd PRE-Cog Sci Workshop (Boston, MA)*.

Hayashi, M. (2004). Projection and grammar: notes on the action-projectinguse of the distal demonstrative are in japanese. *Journal of pragmatics 36*(8), 1337–1374.

Kelleher, J. D. and G.-J. M. Kruijff (2006). Incremental generation of spatial referring expressions in situated dialog. In *Proceedings of the 21st International Conference on Computational Linguistics and the 44th annual meeting of the Association for Computational Linguistics*, pp. 1041–1048. Association for Computational Linguistics.

Kendon, A. (2004). *Gesture: Visible action as utterance*. Cambridge University Press.

Krahmer, E. and I. van der Sluis (2003). A new model for generating multimodal referring expressions. In *Proceedings of the 9th European Workshop on Natural Language Generation (ENLG-2003) at EACL 2003*.

Krishnaswamy, N., S. Friedman, and J. Pustejovsky (2019). Combining Deep Learning and Qualitative Spatial Reasoning to Learn Complex Structures from Sparse Examples with Noise. In *AAAI Conference on Artificial Intelligence (AAAI)*. AAAI.

Krishnaswamy, N., P. Narayana, I. Wang, K. Rim, R. Bangar, D. Patil, G. Mulay, J. Ruiz, R. Beveridge, B. Draper, and J. Pustejovsky (2017). Communicating and acting: Understanding gesture in simulation semantics. In *12th International Workshop on Computational Semantics*.

Krishnaswamy, N. and J. Pustejovsky (2016). Multimodal semantic simulations of linguistically underspecified motion events. In *Spatial Cognition X: International Conference on Spatial Cognition*. Springer.

Krishnaswamy, N. and J. Pustejovsky (2018). An evaluation framework for multimodal interaction. *Proceedings of LREC*.

Lascarides, A. and M. Stone (2006). Formal semantics for iconic gesture. In *Proceedings of the 10th Workshop on the Semantics and Pragmatics of Dialogue (BRANDIAL)*, pp. 64–71.

Lascarides, A. and M. Stone (2009a). Discourse coherence and gesture interpretation. *Gesture 9*(2), 147–180.

Lascarides, A. and M. Stone (2009b). A formal semantic analysis of gesture. *Journal of Semantics*, ffp004.

Latoschik, M. E. and I. Wachsmuth (1997). Exploiting distant pointing gestures for object selection in a virtual environment. In *International Gesture Workshop*, pp. 185–196. Springer.

Meira, S. (2003). addressee effects in demonstrative systems. *Deictic conceptualisation of space, time, and person 112*, 3.

Moratz, R., B. Nebel, and C. Freksa (2002). Qualitative spatial reasoning about relative position. In *International Conference on Spatial Cognition*, pp. 385–400. Springer.

Moratz, R. and T. Tenbrink (2006). Spatial reference in linguistic human-robot interaction: Iterative, empirically supported development of a model of projective relations. *Spatial cognition and computation 6*(1), 63–107.

Narayana, P., N. Krishnaswamy, I. Wang, R. Bangar, D. Patil, G. Mulay, K. Rim, R. Beveridge, J. Ruiz, J. Pustejovsky, and B. Draper (2018). Cooperating with avatars through gesture, language and action. In *Intelligent Systems Conference (IntelliSys)*.

Oviatt, S. (1999). Ten myths of multimodal interaction. *Communications of the ACM 42*(11), 74–81.

Piwek, P., R.-J. Beun, and A. Cremers (2008). proximal and distal in language and cognition: Evidence from deictic demonstratives in dutch. *Journal of Pragmatics 40*(4), 694–718.

Proulx, P. (1988). The demonstrative pronouns of proto-algonquian. *International journal of American linguistics 54*(3), 309–330.

Pustejovsky, J. (2018). From actions to events. *Interaction Studies 19*(1-2), 289–317.

Pustejovsky, J. and N. Krishnaswamy (2016, May). VoxML: A visualization modeling language. In N. C. C. Chair), K. Choukri, T. Declerck, S. Goggi, M. Grobelnik, B. Maegaard, J. Mariani, H. Mazo, A. Moreno, J. Odijk, and S. Piperidis (Eds.), *Proceedings of the Tenth International Conference on Language Resources and Evaluation (LREC 2016)*, Paris, France. European Language Resources Association (ELRA).

Randell, D., Z. Cui, A. Cohn, B. Nebel, C. Rich, and W. Swartout (1992). A spatial logic based on regions and connection. In *KR'92. Principles of Knowledge Representation and Reasoning: Proceedings of the Third International Conference*, San Mateo, pp. 165–176. Morgan Kaufmann.

Schneider, R. (2014). *Convex bodies: the Brunn–Minkowski theory*. Number 151. Cambridge university press.

Skubic, M., D. Perzanowski, S. Blisard, A. Schultz, W. Adams, M. Bugajska, and D. Brock (2004). Spatial language for human-robot dialogs. *Systems, Man, and Cybernetics, Part C: Applications and Reviews, IEEE Transactions on 34*(2), 154–167.

Sluis, I. v. d. and E. Krahmer (2004). The influence of target size and distance on the production of speech and gesture in multimodal referring expressions. In *Eighth International Conference on Spoken Language Processing*.

Strauss, S. (2002). This, that, and it in spoken american english: a demonstrative system of gradient focus. *Language Sciences 24*(2), 131–152.

Viethen, J. and R. Dale (2008). The use of spatial relations in referring expression generation. In *Proceedings of the Fifth International Natural Language Generation Conference*, pp. 59–67. Association for Computational Linguistics.

Volterra, V., M. C. Caselli, O. Capirci, and E. Pizzuto (2005). Gesture and the emergence and development of language. *Beyond nature-nurture: Essays in honor of Elizabeth Bates*, 3–40.

Whitney, D., M. Eldon, J. Oberlin, and S. Tellex (2016). Interpreting multimodal referring expressions in real time. In *Robotics and Automation (ICRA), 2016 IEEE International Conference on*, pp. 3331–3338. IEEE.

On Learning Word Embeddings From Linguistically Augmented Text Corpora

Amila Silva   Chathurika Amarathunga

Singapore Management University

{amilasilva,chathurikaa}@smu.edu.sg

Abstract

Word embedding learning is a technique in Natural Language Processing (NLP) to map words into vector space representations, is one of the most popular research directions in modern NLP by virtue of its potential to boost the performance of many NLP downstream tasks. Nevertheless, most of the underlying word embedding methods such as word2vec and GloVe fail to produce high-quality representations if the text corpus is small and sparse. This paper proposes a method to generate effective word embeddings from limited data. Empirically, we show that the proposed model outperforms existing works for the classical word similarity task and for a domain-specific application.

1 Introduction

Representing words as feature vectors is a vital task in NLP. The trivial approach of representing words as distinct symbols is insufficient since it ignores semantic and syntactic similarities between words. As a result, distributional semantic models (DSMs) of word meanings (Clark, 2012; Erk, 2012) have been emerged, which were built on the hypothesis of *"words with similar meanings tend to appear in similar contexts"* (Harris, 1954). Most of the earliest DSMs for word representation learning are mainly based on clustering (Brown et al., 1992; Kneser and Ney, 1993; Uszkoreit and Brants, 2008) or factorizing (Bullinaria and Levy, 2007; Turney and Pantel, 2010; Baroni and Lenci, 2010; Ritter et al., 2010) global word co-occurrence matrix. However, with the introduction of neural word embedding methods by (Bengio et al., 2003), many studies (Collobert and Weston, 2008; Baroni et al., 2014) empirically prove that neural word embedding methods regularly and substantially outperform traditional DSMs. Thus, various neural models have been proposed recently for word representation learning.

Among the neural word embedding models, word2vec (Mikolov et al., 2013) is widely used in many NLP downstream tasks due to its efficiency in training and scalability. Word2vec learns word representations by maximizing the likelihood of the local context of words (defined using a window around a word). Following the light of word2vec, the variants of word2vec were introduced later with different context definitions. (Levy and Goldberg, 2014) introduced a model in which the contexts are defined by first-order dependency links between words. As extensions to the (Levy and Goldberg, 2014)'s work, (Komninos and Manandhar, 2016; Li et al., 2018) introduced second-order and higher-order dependency-based context for word embedding learning. Nevertheless, none of the existing neural models is capable to capture different types of contexts at once in their models. However, there are previous efforts (Minkov and Cohen, 2008) to design such a model using non-neural approaches.

Although the neural word embedding models have been proven useful in many NLP applications, the existing models have a few limitations. First, the existing works assume that the availability of large corpora, which may not be always available. Especially, the resources are limited to learn domain-specific embedding in most of the cases. Second, even though there are domain adaptation techniques (Bollegala et al., 2015) to overcome the scarcity of domain-specific resources in learning word embedding, it also requires a large amount of data from the source domain. Third, the existing works are only capable to capture one particular context, despite the fact that there are multiple ways to define context (Curran, 2004) using other linguistic relations (i.e., using dependency relations, using co-reference relations).

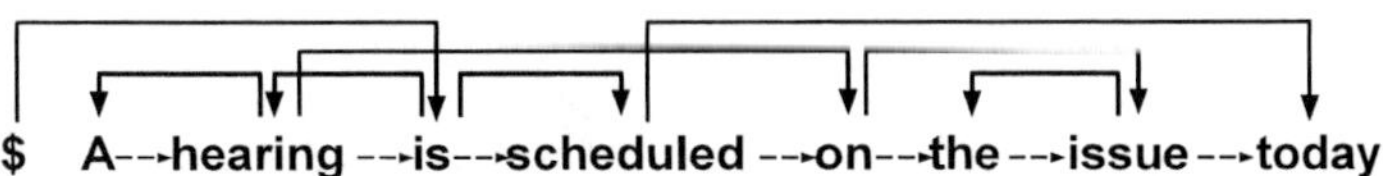

Figure 1: A sentence as a network, each word is a node in the network and edges are obtained from dependency links (solid links) and linear links (dashed links).

To overcome these limitations, here we propose a method to expand the number of sentences in a small text corpus by linguistically generating multiple versions for each sentence. To do so, a network is constructed for each sentence such that different types of context appeared within the neighbourhood of each word in the sentence. Then the multiple versions of the sentence are generated by exploring the linguistic network using a biased random walk approach (discussed in detail in Section 2), motivated by previous network representation learning techniques (Perozzi et al., 2014; Grover and Leskovec, 2016).

The rest of the paper is structured as follows. In Section 2, the technical details of our approach is presented. In Section 3, we evaluate our model using two different tasks and assess the hyperparameter sensitivity of our approach. We conclude the manuscript with some promising directions for future works in Section 4.

2 Proposed Approach

Let us first discuss the word2vec skip-gram model (Mikolov et al., 2013). For a given set of sentences, the skip-gram model loops on the words in each sentence and tries to use the current word to predict its neighbors. Formally, given a sequence of training words $w_1, w_2, w_3, ..., w_T$, the skip-gram model maximizes the following equation,

$$\frac{1}{T} \sum_{t=1}^{T} \sum_{-c \geq j \leq c} log\, p(w_{t+j}|w_t) \tag{1}$$

where c is the window size around the center word. In word2vec, each word-context pair acts as a data point in training. However, if the given corpus is small, it produces only a smaller number of word-context pairs, which might not be enough to train a word2vec model. The intuition behind our model is to generate multiple versions of the same sentence, which captures different contexts in each version and consequently provide more word-context pairs to learn the skip-gram model.

2.1 Random Walks Over Sentences

The contexts defined by a window approach (*linear-based*) and dependency relations (*dependency-based*) are considered within the scope of this paper to construct the linguistic network of a sentence as shown in Figure 1, in which nodes are the words in the sentence and dependency links and linear links create the edges. However, our model can be easily scaled to capture the contexts defined using other linguistic structures such as POS tag and named entity sequences.

We perform random walks of fixed length starting from the first word of each sentence. The formal procedure of random walks is described as follows: Let n_i and n_{i-1} denote the ith and $i-1^{th}$ nodes in the walk and n_i is sampled from the following probability distribution:

$$P(n_i = x | n_{i-1} = y) = \begin{cases} \frac{\pi_{yx}}{Z} & \text{If } (y, x) \, \epsilon \, E \\ 0 & \text{otherwise} \end{cases} \tag{2}$$

where π_{yx} is the unnormalized transition probability between the nodes y and x, Z is the normalizing factor ($Z = \sum_{\forall \, (y,z) \, \epsilon \, E} \pi_{yz}$), and E is the edge list. The transition probabilities (see Section 2.2) between nodes are set in a manner that the multiple random walks of a sentence have different local-contexts in their words. Then the random walks generated for all the sentences are used to train a word2vec model as illustrated in Figure 2.

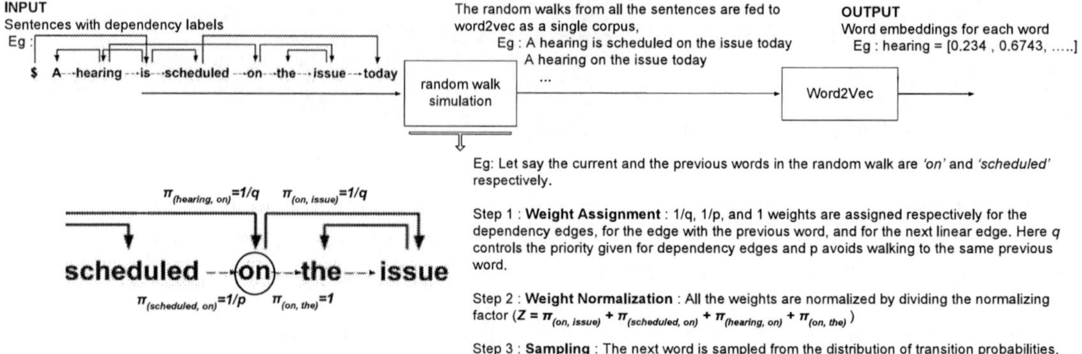

Figure 2: The proposed model for learning word embeddings

2.2 Biasing For Different Contexts

To give different priorities for different edge types, each edge is weighted (w_{yx}) based on the edge type and the nodes are sampled based on the edge weights ($\pi_{yx} = w_{yx}$) as follows; Let x, y, z denote the previous, current, and next words in a random walk respectively.

$$\pi_{yx} = \begin{cases} 1/p & \text{if } x = z \\ 1 & \text{if } (y, z) \in E_{linear} \\ 1/q & \text{if } (y, z) \in E_{dependency} \end{cases} \tag{3}$$

where parameters p and q are the hyperparameters to bias the random walk procedure and $E_{dependency}$ and E_{linear} represent the lists of edges based on dependency and linear links respectively.

By setting a high value for p ($> max(1, q)$), we can avoid the immediate reappearance of same words in random walks. The parameter q controls the priority that is given for the dependency links. If q is high (> 1), priority will be given for the linear edges. In contrast, if q is low (< 1), priority will be given for the dependency based edges. Hence, two extreme cases will be able to capture *linear-based* and *dependency-based* context respectively.

3 Experiments

3.1 Dataset Construction

For the word similarity task, the embeddings were trained on a smaller section of English Wikipedia corpus (Al-Rfou et al., 2013)[1], which contains 1,911,951 sentences, 52,468,613 tokens and 555,688 unique words. In addition, we trained malware-domain specific embeddings using a corpus extracted from APTnotes, a repository of publicly-available papers and blogs related to malicious campaigns, activity, and software [2]. We have chosen 193 reports from the year 2010 to 2015. Since APTnotes are in PDF format, PDFMiner tool (Shinyama, 2004) has been used to convert PDF files into plain text format. After removing the non-sentences, headers, and footers; this malware-related text corpus consists of 27,553 sentences, 108,311 tokens, and 37,857 unique words. Spacy[3] is used to obtain dependency labels for both datasets.

3.2 Baseline Methods

We consider following baseline methods to assess the effectiveness of our approach,

---

[1] https://sites.google.com/site/rmyeid/projects/polyglot
[2] https://github.com/aptnotes/data
[3] https://spacy.io/

Table 1: Results on word similarity/relatedness.

	SVD	W2V	GloVe	Ext	W2V | Ext	GloVe | Ext	Our Model
SIMLEX	0.2611	0.2828	0.2413	0.1531	0.2306	0.2530	**0.2991**
WS-353	0.6055	0.6098	0.5230	0.4532	0.6266	0.5554	**0.6616**
MEN	0.5232	0.5078	0.5799	0.4681	0.5651	0.6069	**0.6293**

- **SVD** (Bullinaria and Levy, 2007): SVD decomposition of the PPMI matrix (Only top 10000 frequent words are considered to generate PPMI matrix due to the computational complexity).

- **word2vec** (Mikolov et al., 2013): The original skip-gram model based on negative sampling.

- **GloVe** (Pennington et al., 2014): This model efficiently leverages global statistical information through factorizing a word-word co-occurrence matrix.

- **Ext** (Komninos and Manandhar, 2016): This model uses dependency based context for learning word embeddings. It introduces second-order dependency into the model proposed by (Levy and Goldberg, 2014).

In addition, the concatenations of linear-context baselines and dependency-context baselines are also considered as a separate set of baselines. For a fair comparison, we set dimension of the embeddings to 300, the number of negative samples to 5, and the context window size to 10 in all the baselines. More details about the experimental setups are discussed in Section 3.3.

3.3 Results

3.3.1 Word Similarity/Relatedness Task

This is a widely used task to evaluate the effectiveness of word embeddings. We use three different datasets, namely: (a) SIMLEX-999 (Hill et al., 2015), (b) WS-353 (Agirre et al., 2009), and (c) MEN (Bruni et al., 2014). Each dataset uses a different notion of word similarity for scoring. The cosine value between two word vectors is used to measure the degree of similarity/relatedness between them. The Spearmans rank correlation coefficient (Myers et al., 2013) is used to check the correlation of ranks between the human annotation and computed similarities. The hyperparameters of the models are tuned using the development set of the MEN dataset. Consequently, 1.5, 1, and 3 are set to p, q, and *number of walks* hyperparameters respectively. The same set of hyperparameter values is used for all the experiments.

According to the results in Table 1, our model outperforms the baselines considerably for all the datasets. Even though the traditional distributional models like SVD have been proven effective for small corpora in some cases, SVD doesn't perform well here. The concatenation of *linear-based* and *dependency-based* baselines shows improvements over their individual models, which further shows the importance of capturing different types of context together in learning embeddings.

Parameter Sensitivity: As shown in Figure 3a, our model considerably outperforms word2vec when the corpus size is small. However, the improvement against word2vec are declined when the corpus grows. This observation clearly supports the fact that our model is especially effective for small corpora. Figure 3b shows the results for different p and q values. In our model, the extreme ends of the scale of q represents the merely *linear-based* ($q >> 1$) and merely *dependency-based* ($q << 1$) systems. Hence, the good performance with the setting of $q = 1$ means that the capturing of both the linear-based and dependency-based contexts together leads to good performance. With this setting, target words of the sentence can access to its local context and dependency context and also to the local context of the dependency related words. This is where our model is superior compared to the computationally expensive method, which enumerate all the possible dependency and linear paths separately.As shown in Figure 3c, we observe that increasing the *number of walks per sentence* improves the performance until the parameter reaches 3. The performance remains consistent for further increments of the parameter.

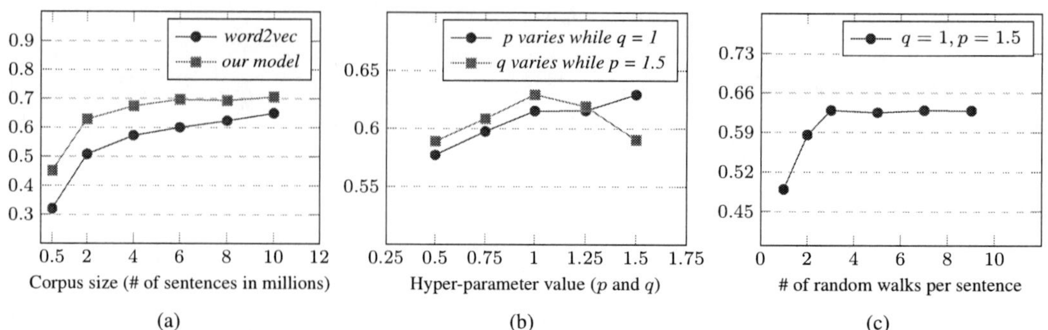

Figure 3: Results (using MEN dataset) for word similarity/relatedness task: (a) for different sizes of the corpora, (b) for different p and q settings, and (c) for different number of random walks per sentence. y axes represent the Spearman's rank correlation coefficient.

Table 2: Results on malware-domain specific sentence classification.

	SVD	W2V	GloVe	Ext	W2V | Ext	GloVe | Ext	Cross-Domain	Our Model
CNN-Static	80.98	81.23	81.94	81.55	80.96	82.43	80.73	**83.12**
CNN-Non-static	81.12	81.42	82.74	82.17	81.45	83.19	80.84	**83.55**

This shows that the use of multiple random walks per sentence leads to capture more useful context of the words, though it is getting saturated after some point.

3.3.2 Malware Related Sentence Classification

In this task, pretrained embeddings are used along with a Convolutional Neural Network (CNN) (Kim, 2014) to perform malware domain-sentence classification task (introduced in SubTask 1 of SemEval-2018 Task 8 - SecureNLP (Phandi et al., 2018)). 10-fold cross-validation is used for the evaluation. Since the domain adaptation techniques have been using to overcome the data constraints in learning domain-specific word embeddings, we consider simple cross-domain word embedding learning baseline in this experiment as an addition. In this baseline, source (Wikipedia corpus) and target (malware corpus) domains are combined to form a single corpus to learn word embeddings.

As shown in Table 2, our approach outperforms other baselines for both CNN-static (embeddings are kept static in training) and CNN-non-static (embeddings are further tuned in training) versions of (Kim, 2014)'s model. Surprisingly, the addition of data from another domain doesn't lead to good performance. Especially, the improvement is significant for CNN-static version, which further shows the quality of the embeddings generated by our model. In addition, the good performance for CNN-non-static version shows that our embeddings are useful for initialization purposes, as pretrained embeddings are only used to initialize word embeddings in the CNN-non-static model.

4 Conclusion

In this paper, we propose a model to capture both *linear* and *dependency-based* contexts together in learning word embeddings. Our model outperforms the well-known baselines for the word similarity task and domain-specific sentence classification task.

Although our model is empirically effective, different types of context (i.e., *dependency-based* and *linear-based*) might not be useful for all the words in learning their representation. Hence more sophisticated walking approach to walk on linguistic structures is worth exploring. Moreover, the combination of other linguistic structures (i.e., co-reference, NER, and POS tag sequences) to the proposed model might be another promising research direction.

References

Agirre, E., E. Alfonseca, K. Hall, J. Kravalova, M. Paşca, and A. Soroa (2009). A study on similarity and relatedness using distributional and wordnet-based approaches. In *Proc. of HLT-NAACL*.

Al-Rfou, R., B. Perozzi, and S. Skiena (2013). Polyglot: Distributed word representations for multilingual nlp. In *Proc. of CoNLL*.

Baroni, M., G. Dinu, and G. Kruszewski (2014). Don't count, predict! a systematic comparison of context-counting vs. context-predicting semantic vectors. In *Proc. of ACL*.

Baroni, M. and A. Lenci (2010). Distributional memory: A general framework for corpus-based semantics. *Computational Linguistics*.

Bengio, Y., R. Ducharme, P. Vincent, and C. Jauvin (2003). A neural probabilistic language model. *Journal of machine learning research*.

Bollegala, D., T. Maehara, and K. ichi Kawarabayashi (2015). Unsupervised cross-domain word representation learning. In *Proc. of ACL*.

Brown, P. F., P. V. Desouza, R. L. Mercer, V. J. D. Pietra, and J. C. Lai (1992). Class-based n-gram models of natural language. *Computational linguistics*.

Bruni, E., N. Tram, M. Baroni, et al. (2014). Multimodal distributional semantics. *The Journal of Artificial Intelligence Research*.

Bullinaria, J. A. and J. P. Levy (2007). Extracting semantic representations from word co-occurrence statistics: A computational study. *Behavior research methods*.

Clark, S. (2012). Vector space models of lexical meaning. *Handbook of Contemporary Semantics–second edition. Wiley-Blackwell*.

Collobert, R. and J. Weston (2008). A unified architecture for natural language processing: Deep neural networks with multitask learning. In *Proc. of ICML*.

Curran, J. R. (2004). From distributional to semantic similarity.

Erk, K. (2012). Vector space models of word meaning and phrase meaning: A survey. *Language and Linguistics Compass*.

Grover, A. and J. Leskovec (2016). node2vec: Scalable feature learning for networks. In *Proc. of ACM SIGKDD*.

Harris, Z. S. (1954). Distributional structure. *Word*.

Hill, F., R. Reichart, and A. Korhonen (2015). Simlex-999: Evaluating semantic models with (genuine) similarity estimation. *Journal of Computational Linguistics*.

Kim, Y. (2014). Convolutional neural networks for sentence classification. In *Proc. of EMNLP*.

Kneser, R. and H. Ney (1993). Improved clustering techniques for class-based statistical language modelling. In *Proc. of EUROSPEECH*.

Komninos, A. and S. Manandhar (2016). Dependency based embeddings for sentence classification tasks. In *Proc. of HLT-NAACL*.

Levy, O. and Y. Goldberg (2014). Dependency-based word embeddings. In *Proc. of ACL*.

Li, C., J. Li, Y. Song, and Z. Lin (2018). Training and evaluating improved dependency-based word embeddings.

Mikolov, T., I. Sutskever, K. Chen, G. S. Corrado, and J. Dean (2013). Distributed representations of words and phrases and their compositionality. In *Proc. of NIPS*.

Minkov, E. and W. W. Cohen (2008). Learning graph walk based similarity measures for parsed text. In *Proc. of EMNLP*.

Myers, J. L., A. D. Well, and R. F. Lorch Jr (2013). *Research design and statistical analysis*. Routledge.

Pennington, J., R. Socher, and C. Manning (2014). Glove: Global vectors for word representation. In *Proc. of EMNLP*.

Perozzi, B., R. Al-Rfou, and S. Skiena (2014). Deepwalk: Online learning of social representations. In *Proc. of ACM SIGKDD*.

Phandi, P., A. Silva, and W. Lu (2018). Semeval-2018 Task 8: Semantic Extraction from CybersecUrity REports using Natural Language Processing (SecureNLP). In *Proc. of SemEval*.

Ritter, A., O. Etzioni, et al. (2010). A latent dirichlet allocation method for selectional preferences. In *Proc. of ACL*.

Shinyama, Y. (2004). PDFMiner. `https:/Interscience/euske.github.io/pdfminer/`.

Turney, P. D. and P. Pantel (2010). From frequency to meaning: Vector space models of semantics. *Journal of artificial intelligence research*.

Uszkoreit, J. and T. Brants (2008). Distributed word clustering for large scale class-based language modeling in machine translation. *Proc. of ACL-08: HLT*.

Sentiment Independent Topic Detection in Rated Hospital Reviews

Christian Wartena
Hochschule Hannover
Christian.Wartena@hs-hannover.de

Uwe Sander
Hochschule Hannover
Uwe.Sander@hs-hannover.de

Christiane Patzelt
Hochschule Hannover
Christiane.Patzelt@hs-hannover.de

Abstract

We present a simple method to find topics in user reviews that accompany ratings for products or services. Standard topic analysis will perform sub-optimal on such data since the word distributions in the documents are not only determined by the topics but by the sentiment as well. We reduce the influence of the sentiment on the topic selection by adding two explicit topics, representing positive and negative sentiment. We evaluate the proposed method on a set of over 15,000 hospital reviews. We show that the proposed method, Latent Semantic Analysis with explicit word features, finds topics with a much smaller bias for sentiments than other similar methods.

1   Introduction

There are many websites that collect user opinions and ratings on products or reviews. In this paper we study a collection of reviews and ratings of orthopedic treatments in hospitals. On the leading German social media website for hospital rating `www.klinikbewertungen.de` users may rate and comment about 3000 hospitals. On this website, in principle it is possible to see what topics are criticized and which ones are valued. To do so, we need to do a topic analysis on the comments.

Since many texts in our corpus have a strong polarity, a standard topic analysis, using Probabilistic Latent Semantic Analysis (PLSA) or Latent Dirichlet Allocation (LDA) also tries to account for the words associated with positive and negative sentiment. Most likely topics and sentiments will be mixed up. E.g. the topic pain is usually associated with negative feelings. Thus negative opinion and pain get mixed up in one topic. Consequently, the topic *Pain* might be found for a document that contains negative words but is not about pain and, vice versa, a document talking about a positive experience on pain treatment will not be associated with the topic *Pain*. Thus we have to model the sentiment and the topic independently.

A straightforward way to make the topic analysis sentiment independent would be to treat comments that come with positive and those that come with negative ratings separately. However, we would end up with incomparable topics for positive and negative comments. Joint topic-sentiment models are designed to find topics and polarity of each document, while we already have the polarity of each document. Moreover, these models are designed to optimize sentiment analysis and not to make the topics less biased towards some sentiment.

The solution we present in Section 2 is basically a simplified formulation of the method proposed by Mei et al. (2007). We use Latent Semantic Analysis (LSA) and add fixed topics for positive and negative sentiment to the set of topics that have to be learned. Thus much of the positive and negative words are explained by these dimensions and less of these words are explained by the other topics.

2   Method

In order to keep the influence of positive or negative opinion out of the topic modeling, we add two fixed topics representing these sentiments to the LSA model. These topics are initialized with values calculated before and not updated in the learning phase. As values for these fixed dimensions we either take the ratings for each document or we compute the polarity of each word.

LSA (Landauer and Dumais, 1997) is a simple but effective method for topic analysis: a term-document matrix is decomposed into two smaller matrices. The rows of the first matrix can be interpreted as the topic distributions of the documents while the second matrix gives the word distribution for these topics. The decomposition is usually realized by Singular Value Decomposition. In the following we will use Non-negative Matrix Factorization (NMF) (Pentti and Unto, 1994) for the decomposition, which makes the weights easier to interpret and can be seen as a variant of PLSA (Hofmann, 2001; Gaussier and Goutte, 2005). We start with the term-document matrix TD of size $m \times n$, with m the number of documents and n the number of terms. Each element $TD_{i,j}$ is the weight of word j for document i. Now we assume that there are k (latent) topics (with $0 < k \ll n$) such that TD can be decomposed into a document-topic matrix U of size $m \times k$ and a word-topic matrix V of size $n \times k$ Since we do not know the topics, we choose some k, initialize U and V randomly and use the stochastic gradient descent algorithm to minimize $||TD - U \cdot V^T||_{Fro^2}$. Furthermore, we require that the row vectors of V^T have magnitude 1.

2.1   LSA with explicit features

As fixed dimensions for positive and negative sentiment we can directly use the given ratings. We initialize the first two columns of U with these values and we will never update these values in the optimization process. Formally, we set

$$
\begin{aligned}
U_{i,0} &= max(0, r_i - 1) \text{ and} & (1) \\
U_{i,1} &= max(0, 2 - r_i) & (2)
\end{aligned}
$$

for each $0 < i \leq m$ where $r_i \in \{0, 1, 2, 3\}$ is the rating associated with document i. We use seperate columns for positive and negative sentiment, since negative sentiment is not just the absence of positive sentiment and neutral words or documents are not words or documents somewhere inbetween positive and negative sentiment, but they are lacking this dimension. We call this method LSA with explicit document features (LSA-ExplDF).

Alternatively, we first determine the positive and negative polarity of each word and initialize the first two columns of V. For this purpose we compute the Information Gain (IG) of every word for the probability function that a document has a positive rating: Let P be a discrete random variable with values 0 and 1 indicating the polarity of the document. Now $H(P)$ is the entropy of P and $H(P \mid w)$ is the relative entropy of P given that it is known whether the word w is in the document. The IG of w is now defined as $I(w) = H(P) - H(P \mid w)$. Finally we set

$$
V_{i,0} = \begin{cases} I(w_i) & \text{if } df(C_{pos}, w) > df(C_{neg}, w) \\ 0 & \text{otherwise} \end{cases} \tag{3}
$$

$$
V_{i,1} = \begin{cases} I(w_i) & \text{if } df(C_{neg}, w) > df(C_{pos}, w) \\ 0 & \text{otherwise} \end{cases} \tag{4}
$$

where $df(C_{neg}, w)$ is the relative document frequency of w in set of all negatively rated documents and $df(C_{pos}, w)$ the relative document frequency of w in set of all positively rated documents. We call this variant LSA with explicit word features (LSA-ExplWF). We implemented the algorithms in Python using the Stochastic Gradient Descent method for NMF from the Scikit-learn package (Pedregosa et al., 2011).

In the following we use LSA-ExplWF and LSA-ExplDF to force the factorization to have dimensions related to positive and negative sentiment. However, we could use the same method for any aspect from the corpus that we want to be represented explicitly, and that should not influence the other topics, like e.g. genre or style.

3 Data

We have tested various topic detection algorithms on reviews from the German platform for hospital reviews, `www.klinikbewertungen.de` (Drevs and Hinz, 2014). Each review consists of five satisfaction scales (overall satisfaction, quality of consultation, medical treatment, administration and procedures, equipment and designing of structures, on a 4-point scale), optional fields for comments about the hospital stay, the pros and cons and the disease pattern in their own words. For our study, in March 2016, we retrieved all reviews for the orthopedics departments. Data collection includes 15,840 reviews of 14,856 patients (93.8%), 852 relatives (4.7%), 30 clinicians/doctors/hospital staff (0.1%) and 102 other affected persons (0.6%) from 1072 hospitals and rehabilitation facilities. 12,098 (76.4%) reviews have positive and 3,742 (23.6%) negative overall rating.

Since in most cases only one text field is filled, we only used the overall rating and concatenated all text fields to one single text. The total number of words in the corpus of these texts is 2,489,356. To construct the term document matrix we lemmatize all words using the Tree Tagger (Schmid, 1994), compute the document frequency and select all nouns and verbs that occur in more than 5 documents and in less than half of all documents. This results in a list of 7,596 words that we use to represent each document. We did not include adjectives and adverbs. These words may also bear topical information but these words are used very frequently to express the sentiment. By excluding these words, we remove already a lot of sentiment from the documents and make the topic detection more neutral with respect to sentiment.

The values of the term-document matrix are the tf.idf values for each term and document. For a corpus C, each term t and document $d \in C$ we define $\mathit{tf.idf}(C, t, d) = \mathit{tf}(t, d) \cdot \mathit{idf}(t)$ with

$$\mathit{tf}(t, d) \;=\; 1 + \log\left(1 + \frac{n(t, d)}{\max_{t' \in V} n(t', d)}\right) \tag{5}$$

$$\mathit{idf}(t, C) \;=\; \log\left(1 + \frac{|C|}{\mathit{df}(C, t)}\right) \tag{6}$$

where V is the vocabulary of C, $n(t, d)$ is the number of occurrences of t in d and $\mathit{df}(C, t)$ is the number of documents in which t occurs. We minimize the effect of the term frequency since the documents that we consider are concatenations of different fields and therefore some words occur more frequently only because it related to an aspect that was asked for in more than one field.

4 Evaluation

We compare three variants: LSA (with NMF), LSA-ExplDF and LSA-ExplWF. In all cases we set the number of topics k to 20 plus the number of fixed topics.

Since the goal is to make the topics independent of the sentiment, we will use exactly this as an evaluation criterion. For each document we determine the two most prominent topics, assuming that there are at least two topics in each text. The results, however, do not depend on the number of topics chosen. Subsequently, we count the number of times each topic is assigned to a negative and to a positive document. If the topics would be completely independent, the ratio of positive and negative documents would be the same for each topic. Thus we take the variance of the fraction of negative documents for each topic as criterion for success: the lower the variance the more independent the topics are from the sentiment. Of course the topics are not independent of the sentiment. Nevertheless a smaller variance indicates that topics ans sentiments are better seperated. Since the results are not deterministic we use averages of 10 runs.

Table 1 gives the average fraction of negative documents and the variance for each method. A lower variance shows that the fraction is more similar for each topic, indicating that the topics are more independent of the sentiment of the texts. We clearly see that LSA-ExplWF give the best result and impressively reduces the variance between the percentage of negative document per topic.

Table 1: Fraction of negative documents per topic.

Method	Average	Variance
LSA	0.25	0.49
LSA-ExplDF	0.26	0.46
LSA-ExplWF	0.25	0.17

Table 2: Most prominent words for all topics found by LSA-ExplWF. Fixed topics are excluded. See Table 3, second column for typical words for the first two topics.

1	sagen, .., tun, gehen, wissen	11	nehmen, zeit, frage, beantworten, erklären
2	reha, therapeut, anwendung, essen, zimmer	12	kind, kur, mutter, kinderbetreuung, tochter
3	operieren, op, operation, hüfte, dr.	13	frau, herr, dr., dank, dr
4	station, schwester, krankenhaus, op, pflegepersonal	14	betreuung, verpflegung, versorgung, unterbringung, behandlung
5	umgebung, schwimmbad, wochenende, nutzen, ort	15	therapie, therapeut, therapieplan, abstimmen, servicepersonal
6	patient, mitarbeiter, freundlichkeit, aufenthalt, kompetenz	16	lws, hws, bandscheibenvorfall, bws, schmerz
7	termin, schmerz, wartezeit, untersuchung, mrt	17	knie, kniegelenk, arthrose, op, tep
8	zimmer, fernseher, internet, telefon, tv	18	tep, hüft, hüfte, ahb, gehhilfen
9	frühstück, abendessen, auswahl, mittagessen, salat	19	wunsch, eingehen, erfüllen, bedürfnis, berücksichtigen
10	massage, vortrag, übung, anwendung, gruppe	20	nicht, und, war, ich, mit

To get an impression of the topics found, Table 2 gives the five most prominent words for each topic found by one run of LSA-ExplWF.

Though the results differ slightly across two runs, most topics are found in each run and many topics found by one method also are found by another method. E.g. both methods find a topic that can be represented by the words *Therapie* (therapy), *Therapeut* (therapist), etc. (topic 15 in Table 2). In the case of LSA this topic was assigned to 888 positive and 569 negative documents. In LSA this topic thus has a strongly negative connotation. Using LSA-ExplWF the topic was assign to 978 positive and 373 negative documents. The comment *"Ich habe mich hier ausgesprochen wohl gefühlt, als ich eine künstliche Hüfte (TEP) erhalten hatte und nach dem Krankenhausaufenthalt drei Wochen in dieser Reha Klinik verbrachte. … Die Therapie wurde ganz individuell auf meine Bedürfnisse abgestimmt. … "* (I felt very well here when I got an artificial hip (TEP) and spent three weeks in the rehabilitation clinic after the hospital stay. … The therapy was individually tailored to my needs. …) got topics 15 and 18 from LSA-ExplWF, while LSA assigned topics 2 and 18, probably because topic 15 has a negative bias in LSA and did not fit for this positive comment. In another example a patient is massively complaining that the doctors did not take time for him, that there was only a standard treatment and he could not shower every day. Here LSA assigns topics 15 and 1, while LSA-ExplWF assigns topics 11 (taking time, answering questions) and 14 (nursing care). LSA probably assigns topic 15 mainly because the text is extremely negative, while LSA-ExplWF precisely identifies the topics that frustrated the patient.

Table 3 gives the most prominent words for the first two topics. Interestingly, the word *empfehlen)* (recommend) is found both for positive and negative sentiment: this word is used in stronly polarized contexts, both with positive and with negative sentiment, but it is not used frequently in neutral reviews.

5 Related Work

Much work on topic detection in combination with sentiment analysis was done on product reviews. The semi-supervised model of McAuliffe and Blei (2008) optimizes the topics for rating prediction. Besides the rated products there are aspects of these products that are discussed positively and negatively. Titov

Table 3: Positive and negative words in LSA-ExplDF and LSA-ExplWF.

	LSA-ExplDF	LSA-ExplWF
	personal *(staff)*	team
	empfehlen *(recommend)*	dank *(thanks)*
+	essen *(meal)*	fühlen *(feel)*
	top	bedanken *(to thank)*
	super	aufheben *(to save)*
	arzt *(doctor)*	katastrophe
	katastrophe	aussage *(statement)*
-	patient	ignorieren *(to ignore)*
	empfehlen *(recommend)*	nachfrage *(demand)*
	geld *(money)*	geld *(money)*

and McDonald (2008) use the same type of data we have. They consider the problem that ratings are given on several aspects but only one textual comment is given. This is also the case for our data. However, they distinguish between global topics and local topics that correspond to ratable aspects of the global topics. They propose an extension of Latent Dirichlet Allocation (LDA) to handle this mixture of global and local topics. In our data, that are much more specific, we did not find such a division between global and local topics and the global topics correspond very well to ratable aspects. Zhao et al. (2010) propose an extension of this model that is able to use various features of words and can distinguish aspect from opinion words.

Much work was done on developing joint topic-sentiment models, usually to improve sentiment detection. Lin and He (2009) propose a method based on LDA that explicitly deals with the interaction of topics and sentiments in text. However, their goal is exactly opposite to ours: they use the fact that the topic distribution is different for positive and negative documents and in fact use the polarity of topics to enhance the sentiment detection, which is the main goal of their efforts. Thus the algorithm is encouraged to find topics that have a high sentiment bias. The joint topic sentiment model of Eguchi and Lavrenko (2006) goes into the same directions: they optimize sentiment detection using the fact that the polarity of words depends on the topic. Also the paper of Maas et al. (2011) follows this general direction. Paul and Dredze (2012) propose a multidimensional model with word distributions for each topic-sentiment combination. This model was used to analyze patient reviews by Wallace et al. (2014).

The work of Mei et al. (2007) is most similar to our approach. In fact our method can be interpreted as a simplification of their method. A difference is that Mei et al. use a background word distribution that is topic and sentiment independent to account for general English words. We also tried this, but such a component did not have any effect. This can be explained by the fact that we removed stop words and used tf.idf weights instead of raw counts. One of their goals also is to avoid a contamination of topics with sentiments. However, they did not evaluate this aspect. Thus the contribution of this paper is not just a simpler formulation of the basic idea of Mei et al. (2007), but also shows that the topics found indeed are less contaminated by sentiment words and less biased towards one sentiment.

6   Discussion

The proposed method gives a simple but effective way to find topics in strongly polarized texts if the polarity of the texts is known, as usually is the case in comments given in rating portals. We have shown on a realistic data set, that the topics found become more independent from the sentiment. We could also show the effect of our method on a few example texts.

Patient comments often have different opinions on different topics. For future work we will try to find out for each comment the topics it is discussing positively and negatively.

References

Drevs, F. and V. Hinz (2014). Who chooses, who uses, who rates: The impact of agency on electronic word-of-mouth about hospitals stays. *Health care management review 39*(3), 223–233.

Eguchi, K. and V. Lavrenko (2006). Sentiment retrieval using generative models. In *Proceedings of the 2006 Conference on Empirical Methods in Natural Language Processing*, pp. 345–354. Association for Computational Linguistics.

Gaussier, E. and C. Goutte (2005). Relation between plsa and nmf and implications. In *Proceedings of the 28th Annual International ACM SIGIR Conference on Research and Development in Information Retrieval*, SIGIR '05, New York, NY, USA, pp. 601–602. ACM.

Hofmann, T. (2001, Jan). Unsupervised learning by probabilistic latent semantic analysis. *Machine Learning 42*(1), 177–196.

Landauer, T. K. and S. T. Dumais (1997). A solution to plato's problem: The latent semantic analysis theory of acquisition, induction, and representation of knowledge. *Psychological Review 104*(2), 211.

Lin, C. and Y. He (2009). Joint sentiment/topic model for sentiment analysis. In *CIKM*.

Maas, A. L., R. E. Daly, P. T. Pham, D. Huang, A. Y. Ng, and C. Potts (2011). Learning word vectors for sentiment analysis. In *Proceedings of the 49th Annual Meeting of the Association for Computational Linguistics: Human Language Technologies - Volume 1*, HLT '11, Stroudsburg, PA, USA, pp. 142–150. Association for Computational Linguistics.

McAuliffe, J. D. and D. M. Blei (2008). Supervised topic models. In *Advances in neural information processing systems*, pp. 121–128.

Mei, Q., X. Ling, M. Wondra, H. Su, and C. Zhai (2007). Topic sentiment mixture: Modeling facets and opinions in weblogs. In *Proceedings of the 16th International Conference on World Wide Web*, WWW '07, New York, NY, USA, pp. 171–180. ACM.

Paul, M. and M. Dredze (2012). Factorial lda: Sparse multi-dimensional text models. In *Advances in Neural Information Processing Systems*, pp. 2582–2590.

Pedregosa, F., G. Varoquaux, A. Gramfort, V. Michel, B. Thirion, O. Grisel, M. Blondel, P. Prettenhofer, R. Weiss, V. Dubourg, et al. (2011). Scikit-learn: Machine learning in python. *Journal of machine learning research 12*(Oct), 2825–2830.

Pentti, P. and T. Unto (1994). Positive matrix factorization: A non-negative factor model with optimal utilization of error estimates of data values. *Environmetrics 5*(2), 111–126.

Schmid, H. (1994). Probabilistic Part-of-Speech Tagging Using Decision Trees. In *International Conference on New Methods in Language Processing*, Manchester, UK, pp. 44–49.

Titov, I. and R. McDonald (2008). A joint model of text and aspect ratings for sentiment summarization. In *Proceedings of ACL-08: HLT*, pp. 308–316. Association for Computational Linguistics.

Wallace, B. C., M. J. Paul, U. Sarkar, T. A. Trikalinos, and M. Dredze (2014). A large-scale quantitative analysis of latent factors and sentiment in online doctor reviews. *Journal of the American Medical Informatics Association: JAMIA 21*(6), 1098–1103.

Zhao, W. X., J. Jiang, H. Yan, and X. Li (2010). Jointly modeling aspects and opinions with a maxent-lda hybrid. In *Proceedings of the 2010 Conference on Empirical Methods in Natural Language Processing*, EMNLP '10, Stroudsburg, PA, USA, pp. 56–65. Association for Computational Linguistics.

Investigating the Stability of Concrete Nouns in Word Embeddings

Bénédicte Pierrejean
Ludovic Tanguy
CLLE: CNRS & University of Toulouse
Toulouse, France
{benedicte.pierrejean,ludovic.tanguy}@univ-tlse2.fr

Abstract

We know that word embeddings trained using neural-based methods (such as word2vec SGNS) are sensitive to stability problems and that across two models trained using the exact same set of parameters, the nearest neighbors of a word are likely to change. All words are not equally impacted by this internal instability and recent studies have investigated features influencing the stability of word embeddings. This stability can be seen as a clue for the reliability of the semantic representation of a word. In this work, we investigate the influence of the degree of concreteness of nouns on the stability of their semantic representation. We show that for English generic corpora, abstract words are more affected by stability problems than concrete words. We also found that to a certain extent, the difference between the degree of concreteness of a noun and its nearest neighbors can partly explain the stability or instability of its neighbors.

1 Introduction

Word embeddings are more and more used in corpus linguistics studies to draw conclusions on the usage of a word. Looking at a word's nearest neighbors in embeddings models is a common way to do that. Word2vec (Mikolov et al., 2013) quickly became one of the most popular tools to train word embeddings since it is easy and convenient to use and yields state of the arts results. Word2vec, like any other neural-based method, implies several random processes when preprocessing the data used for training (subsampling of the corpus) and training word embeddings (initialization of neural networks weights, dynamic window, negative sampling). As a consequence training several times using the same controllable hyperparameters (number of dimensions, window size etc.) will not yield identical models.

Although this instability is not critical when using embeddings in deep learning models for NLP applications, concerns have been raised regarding the use of word embeddings in digital humanities. Observations made by looking at nearest neighbors of a specific word might not be accurate since the nearest neighbors of a word might change from one model to the other. Recently, several studies have investigated the stability of word embeddings and the possible ways to overcome the instability triggered by word embeddings to be able to use them in digital humanities. Hellrich and Hahn (2016) studied the influence of training methods and hyperparameters on this instability. They showed that an accurate selection of the number of training epochs would help prevent the unreliability of word embeddings while preventing overfitting on the training data. Antoniak and Mimno (2018) examined the influence of the corpus used when training word embeddings and showed that embeddings are not a "a single objective view of a corpus". They also emphasized the importance of taking variability into account when observing words' nearest neighbors and showed that the size of the corpus used for training will also influence this variability, in the sense that smaller corpora trigger more variability. A good yet expensive way to overcome this variability would be to draw conclusions from several word embeddings sets trained using the same controllable parameters to confirm the observations made. Other studies investigated the influence of several features on the instability of word embeddings. Wendlandt et al.

(2018) showed that several factors contributed to the instability of word embeddings, POS being one of the most important one, and that unlike what could be expected frequency did not play a major role in the stability of word embeddings. Pierrejean and Tanguy (2018b) investigated the influence of several features that were intrinsic to a word, corpus or model on the stability of word embeddings. They proposed a technique to predict the variation of a word given simple features (POS, degree of polysemy of a word, frequency, entropy of a word with its contexts, norm of the vectors and score of the nearest neighbor of a word). They showed that the cosine similarity score of the nearest neighbor and the POS play a major role in the prediction of the variation. They also showed that words with very low or very high frequency are more affected by variation. Pierrejean and Tanguy (2018a) also identified some semantic clusters that would remain stable from one model to the other when training word embeddings using the same controllable hyperparameters. Most of these clusters seem to consist of concrete words (e.g. family members, objects and rooms of the house).

Some recent works studied the semantic representations of concrete and abstract words in count-based distributional models and showed that concrete words have concrete nearest neighbors while abstract words tend to have abstract nearest neighbors (Frassinelli et al., 2017). Naumann et al. (2018) also showed that abstract words have higher contextual variability and are thus more difficult to predict than concrete words. We wonder if those findings would also apply to models trained using neural-based methods and if different behaviors regarding variability could be observed for concrete and abstract words.

In this work we analyze the relationship between the variation of nearest neighbors of a noun and its degree of concreteness. In order to get a good understanding of this relationship, we decided to perform our analysis on 4 corpora of different sizes and types. First, we investigate the relationship existing between the variation of nearest neighbors and frequency. Then we investigate the impact of the degree of concreteness of a noun on the stability of its semantic representation. Finally, we analyze the stability of the nearest neighbors of nouns through their degree of concreteness.

2   Experiment setup

2.1   Models

We trained word embeddings using word2vec (Mikolov et al., 2013) on 4 corpora of different sizes and types. We used 2 generic corpora, the BNC made of about 100 million words[1], and UMBC, a web-based corpus made of about 3 billion words (Han et al., 2013). We also used 2 specialized corpora, ACL (NLP scientific papers from the ACL Anthology (Bird et al., 2008)) made of about 100 million words, and PLOS also consisting of about 100 million words (biology scientific papers gathered from the PLOS archive collections[2]). Corpora were lemmatized and POS-tagged using the Talismane toolkit (Urieli, 2013). For each corpus, we trained 5 models using the same following default hyperparameters: architecture Skip-Gram with negative sampling rate of 5, window size set to 5, vectors dimensions set to 100, subsampling rate set to 10^{-3} and number of iterations set to 5. We only considered words that appear more than 100 times.

2.2   Word-level variation

Computing the variation of nearest neighbors is an easy way to assess the quality of a semantic representation. Nearest neighbors that remain the same from one model to the other can be considered more reliable than neighbors that vary. To measure this we computed the degree of variation for the 25 nearest neighbors of a word between two models. The variation score corresponds to the ratio of nearest neighbours that do not appear in both models (without considering their rank). E.g., a variation score of 0.20 indicates than for the 25 nearest neighbors of a word in one model, 5 neighbors do not appear in the 25 nearest neighbors of the other model. We performed pairwise comparisons between the 5 trained models

---

[1] http://www.natcorp.ox.ac.uk/
[2] www.plos.org

for each corpus resulting in 10 comparisons per corpus. We computed the variation for a selected set of POS only: nouns, adjectives, verbs and adverbs. We then computed the mean variation for each word.

2.3   Concreteness

Following Naumann et al. (2018) we used the concreteness ratings presented by Brysbaert et al. (2014). Those ratings were collected using crowdsourcing. 40 000 words total were rated between 1 (abstract word) to 5 (concrete words). The instructions given to participants stated that the concreteness of a word is defined as "something you can experience through your senses". The resource contains 14 592 nouns that have an average concreteness score of 3.53 ($\pm$1.02).

Using this resource, each noun in each corpus was given a concreteness score. We excluded other POS since as it was noted by Frassinelli et al. (2017), it is easier to qualify the degree of concreteness of nouns. In the analyses performed using the degree of concreteness, we only considered words existing in the resource. This resulted in 8 796 nouns for the BNC, 5 288 nouns for PLOS, 19 720 nouns for UMBC and 3 899 nouns for ACL. We computed the average concreteness of these nouns for each corpus. This resulted in an average concreteness score of 3.38 for UMBC ($\pm$1.01), 3.48 for the BNC ($\pm$1.02), 3.28 for ACL ($\pm$1.01) and 3.47 for PLOS ($\pm$0.98).

3   Results

3.1   Intrinsic evaluation

To check the overall performance of our models, we ran an intrinsic evaluation using a standard evaluation test set, MEN (Bruni et al., 2013). MEN consists of 3000 pairs of words. Some words used in MEN pairs are not present in the different models vocabulary. Thus the evaluation was run on 1 176 pairs for ACL, 2 687 pairs for the BNC, 1 516 pairs for PLOS and 2 996 pairs for UMBC. We reported the average score (Spearman correlation) for the 5 models for each corpus in Table 1. We can see that results are different for all corpora. Generic corpora have higher scores (0.73 for the BNC and 0.70 for UMBC) compared to specialized corpora (0.51 for ACL and 0.57 for PLOS). This is not surprising because the type of evaluation test set we used is not really tailored for small specialized corpora such as ACL and PLOS.

We observed that the results were quite stable across models. As a side note, it is important to mention that most of the nouns in the MEN test set are concrete nouns with an average concreteness score of 4.6. This raises questions regarding the bias of intrinsic evaluation test sets. When evaluating distributional semantics models, what does it mean to focus mainly on evaluating the semantic representation of concrete words? If we consider word embeddings more particularly and the fact that they are prone to stability problems, how does the stability relate to the concreteness of a word? Are concrete words more stable than abstract words? We propose to investigate those effects in the following experiments.

Corpus	MEN score	Voc. size	Mean variation	Std. dev. (models)	Std. dev. (words)
ACL	0.51	22 292	0.16	0.04	0.08
BNC	0.73	27 434	0.17	0.04	0.08
PLOS	0.57	31 529	0.18	0.05	0.09
UMBC	0.70	184 396	0.22	0.05	0.10

Table 1: MEN score, vocabulary size, mean variation score and standard deviations for each corpus (5 models trained per corpus).

3.2   Global variation

To get an estimate of the proportion of instability in our models, we started by computing the variation of the 25 nearest neighbors for every word in each corpus.

Table 1 displays the vocabulary size for models trained for each corpus as well as the mean variation along with standard deviation. The variation is very similar from one corpus to the other. Standard deviation is low (average of 0.04) across the 10 pairs of models, meaning that the variation is equally distributed among the comparisons made for each corpus. The standard deviation across words is twice as high (average of 0.09), which indicates that there are important differences in variation from one word to the other within the same category of models.

We wish to investigate the correlation between the variation score of a word and its degree of concreteness. A positive correlation would confirm that concrete words have a better semantic representation.

3.3 Frequency

Before looking at the impact of concreteness on variation, we need to understand the relationship between variation and frequency. As we can see in Table 2, variation and frequency are correlated in all our corpora. We see that less frequent words tend to vary less. This effect is clearer for specialized corpora. However we observed that the relation between variation and frequency is not linear with words in very low or high frequency range having a tendency to vary more than words in the mid-frequency range. This is partly in line with Sahlgren and Lenci (2016) who observed that it is more challenging for neural-based models to train good vectors for low-frequency words.

Corpus	Number of nouns	Nouns with concr. score	Correl. freq-var	Correl. freq-concr.	Correl. var-concr.
ACL	5 534	3 899	-0.42	-0.12	+0.10
BNC	10 266	8 796	-0.15	+0.03	-0.16
PLOS	9 751	5 288	-0.26	-0.07	+0.01 (ns)
UMBC	49 141	19 720	-0.27	-0.07	-0.16

Table 2: Spearman correlation scores between frequency and variation, frequency and degree of concreteness and variation and degree of concreteness. All correlations scores are significant at the 0.05 level except for the one where ns is indicated.

3.4 Concreteness and variation

We wanted to know if the degree of concreteness of a noun also has an impact on the variation of its nearest neighbors. We first wanted to confirm that distributionally similar words have similar concreteness scores (Frassinelli et al., 2017). To do so we selected the 1000 most concrete and 1000 most abstract nouns in the BNC. For each noun, we computed the average concreteness score of nearest neighbors that were nouns amongst its 25 nearest neighbors. We found that neighbors of concrete nouns had an average concreteness score of 4.6 and nearest neighbors of abstract nouns had an average concreteness score of 2.37 meaning that distributionally similar words do have similar concreteness scores.

We then investigated the correlation between the frequency of a noun and its degree of concreteness. As we can see in Table 2 the effect of frequency is almost null for the BNC. However we observe a weak negative correlation for ACL, PLOS and UMBC with less frequent words being more concrete.

We computed the correlation between the variation score of nouns and their degree of concreteness. We reported the results in Table 2. We observed different behaviors for the different corpora. We found that abstract words have a clear tendency to vary more in generic corpora (BNC and UMBC) with a Spearman correlation of -0.16. In the BNC, words such as *kitchen*, *wife*, *sitting-room* or *grandmother* are concrete and have a low variation score. These words correspond to the clusters identified by Pierrejean and Tanguy (2018a). On the other side of the spectrum, we found words like *legacy*, *realization*, *succession* or *coverage* that are abstract and whose neighbors vary significantly.

Things are very different for specialized corpora. While the effect is not visible in PLOS, the opposite effect is observed in ACL with a positive correlation. Concrete words such as *carrot*, *turtle*, *umbrella* or *horse* vary a lot. These words have a low frequency in the corpus (around 100 occurrences) and correspond to words that are used in examples. This also explains the higher negative correlation between concreteness and frequency in ACL. Abstract words in ACL correspond to words that are very stable across the different models, e.g. *recall*, *precision* or *pre-processing*.

This difference in behavior observed between specialized and non-specialized corpora is not surprising since we use a resource where concreteness was defined as something you can experience through your senses. This raises questions concerning the notion of concreteness and what it means for a word to be concrete in a specialized corpus. It seems very important to consider the nature of the corpus when performing this type of experiments and to take into consideration that changing corpus equals to changing world. This question is especially crucial when working in specialized domains where the quantity of available data might be limited.

3.5 Concreteness of nearest neighbors and stability

We saw that nearest neighbors of a word tend to have a similar degree of concreteness. As we mentioned before, for a given word, amongst its nearest neighbors some will remain stable from one model to the other while others will vary. Here we propose to investigate the interaction between the degree of concreteness of the nearest neighbor of a noun and its stability. For the following experiments we chose to focus only on the BNC.

First for each noun we retrieved the union of its 25 nearest neighbors in the 5 models trained for each corpus. We only kept nearest neighbors that were nouns. For each nearest neighbor we retrieved its degree of concreteness when available in the resource we previously used. We also computed its cosine similarity with the target word in each model. We then computed the absolute difference between the degree of concreteness of the target and the degree of concreteness of the given neighbor as well as the standard deviation of the cosine scores across the 5 different models.

Then for each concrete noun (with a degree of concreteness above 4.2) we computed the Spearman correlation between the absolute difference of concreteness and the standard deviation of the cosines.

For the BNC, we found that in 65% of the cases where the correlation is significant the correlation is positive. This means that the higher the difference between the concreteness score of a target word with one of its neighbor, the more likely this neighbor is to change from one model to the other. For example, for the noun *telescope* (concr. = 5), two close neighbors like *wavelength* (concr. = 3.35) and *lens* (concr. = 4.64) have very similar average cosine scores with *telescope* (0.67 and 0.62 resp.). However the similarity score of *telescope* with the more abstract neighbor of the two (*wavelength*) displays much more variation across the 5 models (0.013 and 0.005 resp.).

This effect is less visible for more abstract target nouns. Amongst the significant correlations the positive ones are always more frequent but their proportion is lower for abstract words (down to 52% positive correlations).

4 Conclusion

We further explored the relation between concreteness and word embeddings. We already knew that concrete words have concrete nearest neighbors. We found that concrete words also present less instability problems and frequency by itself does not explain this phenomenon. Similarly, abstract words show more variation in their neighbors across distributional models. This indicates that word embeddings are more reliable for concrete words. Interestingly, evaluation test sets such as MEN consist mainly of concrete words.

Further investigations are required to fully understand the influence of the degree of concreteness of words. However, we can state that for extremely concrete words, nearest neighbors having a similar degree of concreteness with their target are the most stable.

The above results were found only in generic corpora (BNC and UMBC) and we observed the opposite effect – or no effect at all – in specialized corpora (ACL and PLOS). This is partly due to the fact that the way concreteness is defined in generic resources is not relevant for specialized corpora. Even though this work provided several elements to better understand the stability of word embeddings, we still need to investigate factors influencing the stability of word embeddings as well as their reliability.

References

Antoniak, M. and D. Mimno (2018). Evaluating the stability of embedding-based word similarities. *Transactions of the Association for Computational Linguistics 6*, 107–119.

Bird, S., R. Dale, B. Dorr, B. Gibson, M. Joseph, M.-Y. Kan, D. Lee, B. Powley, D. Radev, and Y. Fan Tan (2008). The ACL Anthology Reference Corpus: A Reference Dataset for Bibliographic Research in Computational Linguistics. In *Proceedings of Language Resources and Evaluation Conference (LREC 08)*.

Bruni, E., N.-K. Tran, and M. Baroni (2013). Multimodal Distributional Semantics. *Journal of Artificial Intelligence Research 49*, 1–47.

Brysbaert, M., A. B. Warriner, and V. Kuperman (2014). Concreteness ratings for 40 thousand generally known Enlish word lemmas. *Behavior Research Methods 46*, 904–911.

Frassinelli, D., D. Naumann, J. Utt, and S. Schulte im Walde (2017). Contextual Characteristics of Concrete and Abstract Words. In *IWCS 2017 - 12th International Conference on Computational Semantics - Short papers*.

Han, L., A. L. Kashyap, T. Finin, J. Mayfield, and J. Weese (2013). UMBC EBIQUITY-CORE: Semantic Textual Similarity Systems. In *Proc. 2nd Joint Conference on Lexical and Computational Semantics, Association for Computational Linguistics*.

Hellrich, J. and U. Hahn (2016). Bad Company - Neighborhoods in Neural Embedding Spaces Considered Harmful. In *Proceedings of COLING 2016, the 26th International Conference on Computational Linguistics: Technical Papers*, Osaka, Japan, pp. 2785–2796.

Mikolov, T., I. Sutskever, K. Chen, G. Corrado, and J. Dean (2013). Distributed Representations of Words and Phrases and their Compositionality. *arXiv:1310.4546 [cs, stat]*.

Naumann, D., D. Frassinelli, and S. Schulte im Walde (2018). Quantitative Semantic Variation in the Contexts of Concrete and Abstract Words. In *Proceedings of the 7th Joint Conference on Lexical and Computational Semantics (*SEM)*, New Orleans, pp. 76–85.

Pierrejean, B. and L. Tanguy (2018a). Étude de la reproductibilité des word embeddings : repérage des zones stables et instables dans le lexique. In *TALN*, Rennes, France.

Pierrejean, B. and L. Tanguy (2018b). Predicting word embeddings variability. In *Proceedings of the 7th Joint Conference on Lexical and Computational Semantics (*SEM)*, New Orleans, pp. 154–159.

Sahlgren, M. and A. Lenci (2016). The Effects of Data Size and Frequency Range on Distributional Semantic Models. In *Proceedings of the 2016 Conference on Empirical Methods in Natural Language Processing*, Austin, Texas, pp. 975–980.

Urieli, A. (2013). *Robust French syntax analysis: reconciling statistical methods and linguistic knowledge in the Talismane toolkit*. Ph. D. thesis, Université Toulouse-II Le Mirail.

Wendlandt, L., J. K. Kummerfeld, and R. Mihalcea (2018). Factors Influencing the Surprising Instability of Word Embeddings. In *Proceedings of NAACL-HLT 2018*, New Orleans, pp. 2092–2102.

Association for Computational Linguistics
209 N. Eighth Street
Stroudsburg, Pennsylvania 18360